EUROPE/AMERICA
7

Europe, America and South Africa

EUROPE/AMERICA 7

Europe, America and South Africa

Francis Pym
Max van der Stoel
Claude Cheysson
Herman W. Nickel
Donald F. McHenry

Gregory F. Treverton, Editor

A Council on Foreign Relations
58 East 68th Street, New York, NY 10021

COUNCIL ON FOREIGN RELATIONS BOOKS

The Council on Foreign Relations, Inc., is a nonprofit and nonpartisan organization devoted to promoting improved understanding of international affairs through the free exchange of ideas. The Council does not take any position on questions of foreign policy and has no affiliation with, and receives no funding from, the United States government.

From time to time, books and monographs written by members of the Council's research staff or visiting fellows, or commissioned by the Council, or written by an independent author with critical review by a Council study or working group are published with the designation "Council on Foreign Relations Book." Any book or monograph bearing that designation is, in the judgment of the Committee on Studies of the Council's board of directors, a responsible treatment of a significant international topic worthy of presentation to the public. All statements of fact and expressions of opinion contained in Council books are, however, the sole responsibility of the author.

First published in hard cover by New York University Press, Washington Square, New York, N.Y. 10033

LIBRARY OF CONGRESS
Library of Congress Cataloging-in-Publication Data

Europe, America and South Africa / Gregory F. Treverton, editor; [contributors] Francis Pym . . . [et al.].
    p.   cm. — (Europe/America ; 7)
Bibliography: p.
   ISBN 0-81479-8180-2
   1. South Africa—Politics and government—1978- 2. South Africa—Foreign public opinion. 3. United States—Relations—Europe.
4. Europe—Relations—United States. 5. North Atlantic Treaty Organization. I. Treverton, Gregory, F. II. Pym, Francis.
III. Series.

The Project on European-American Relations

Relations between Western Europe and the United States have become more turbûlent in recent years. Divergences in interests and perceptions have grown. Many are questioning the fundamental assumptions of the postwar period. There is a broad consensus that the European-American relationship is in a state of transition.

A new generation is emerging and a number of social and cultural changes are under way that are also contributing to this transition. While our common heritage and values set limits on how far we may drift apart, there is an increasing recognition of the divergences between the United States and Europe on such critical issues as defense and arms control, policy toward the Soviet Union, East-West trade and technology transfer, West-West economic relations, North-South issues, and problems outside the NATO area. The challenge for statesmen will be to manage the differences—and where possible create a new Western consensus—in such a way as to enable the Alliance to adapt to new circumstances while preserving its basic character.

The relatively simple world of the postwar period is gone. Americans today appear to have less understanding of European perspectives and Europeans less appreciation of American views. There is much handwringing about the trans-Atlantic malaise, but less constructive thinking about how to manage and, where possible, reduce our differences.

The project is designed to identify and clarify the differences in interests and perspectives affecting critical issues in the European-American relationship, thereby enhancing understanding across the Atlantic. Approximately three issues per year will be selected for examination on a rolling basis over the next three years. The issues will be those that are most likely to create friction in the period ahead.

A short book is published on each issue. European and American authors with points of view that differ from each other but represent important strands of thought in their respective societies will contribute analyses of the problem and offer their policy prescriptions. We hope that by disaggregating the issues in this manner, we can make a constructive contribution to the Atlantic debate.

An advisory group of Council members, with the participation of European guests, will help choose the issues and will discuss the ideas in the manuscripts prior to publication. They are, however, in no way responsible for the conclusions, which are solely those of the authors.

We would like to thank the Rockefeller Foundation, the Andrew W. Mellon Foundation, the German Marshall Fund of the United States and the Ford Foundation for their assistance in supporting this project.

Cyrus R. Vance

Advisory Group
Project on European-American Relations

Cyrus R. Vance, *Chairman*
Robert D. Hormats, *Vice Chairman*
Gregory F. Treverton, *Director of Project*
Steven J. Monde, *Assistant to the Director*

David Aaron
George W. Ball
Seweryn Bialer
John Brademas
Hodding Carter, III
Robert F. Ellsworth
Murray H. Finley
Richard N. Gardner
Stanley Hoffmann
Robert E. Hunter
Irving Kristol
Jan M. Lodal
Charles S. Maier
Robert S. McNamara
Harald B. Malmgren
Maynard Parker
William R. Pearce

Robert V. Roosa
Nathaniel Samuels
J. Robert Schaetzel
John W. Seigle
Marshall D. Shulman
Robert B. Silvers
Anthony M. Solomon
Helmut Sonnenfeldt
Joan E. Spero
Ronald Steel
Fritz Stern
John R. Stevenson
John H. Watts, III

William H. Gleysteen, *ex officio*
Peter Tarnoff, *ex officio*

vii

The editor would like to thank Millard W. Arnold, Pauline Baker, James E. Baker, Philip L. Christenson, Michael Clough, and Milfred C. Fierce and John Stremlau for their assistance in planning and/or commenting on the manuscripts. He would also like to thank Jeremy Brenner, Stephanie Hoelscher, David Kellogg and Steven Monde for their assistance in the production of this book.

The Project on European-American Relations is under the auspices of the Council's Studies Program.

Already published:

Nuclear Weapons in Europe, edited by Andrew J. Pierre, with contributions by William G. Hyland, Lawrence D. Freedman, Paul C. Warnke and Karsten D. Voigt.

Unemployment and Growth in the Western Economies, edited by Andrew J. Pierre, with contributions by Marina v.N. Whitman, Raymond Barre, James Tobin and Shirley Williams, and an introduction by Robert D. Hormats.

Third World Instability: Central America as a European-American Issue, edited by Andrew J. Pierre, with contributions by Fernando Moran, Irving Kristol, Michael D. Barnes, Alois Mertes and Daniel Oduber.

A Widening Atlantic?: Domestic Change and Foreign Policy, edited by Andrew J. Pierre, with contributions by Ralf Dahrendorf and Theodore C. Sorensen.

The Conventional Defense of Europe: New Technologies and New Strategies, edited by Andrew J. Pierre, with contributions by Andrew J. Pierre, Richard D. DeLauer, François L. Heisbourg, Andreas von Bülow and General Sir Hugh Beach.

A High Technology Gap? Europe, America and Japan, edited by Andrew J. Pierre, with contributions by Frank Press, Hubert Curien, Carlo De Benedetti and Keichi Oshima, and an introduction by Robert D. Hormats.

Contents

About the Authors

Claude Cheysson is Commissioner of the European Communities responsible for Mediterranean policy and North-South relations. Previously, from 1973 to 1981, he held the post of EC Commissioner for Developmental Aid. He has served the French government as Minister for External Relations from 1981 to 1984, and as Ambassador to Indonesia from 1966 to 1969. Earlier in his career, Mr. Cheysson was Secretary General of the Commission for Technical Cooperation in Africa, and Director-General of the Sahara Authority.

Donald F. McHenry is University Research Professor of Diplomacy and International Relations at Georgetown University's School of Foreign Service and President of International Relations Consultants, Inc. During the Carter Administration, he served as U.S. Deputy Representative to the UN Security Council from 1977 to 1979, and as Ambassador to the UN from 1979 to 1981. Previously he worked in the state department as an International Affairs Officer, Officer-in-Charge of Dependent Area Affairs, Assistant to the Secretary, and Special Assistant to the Counselor. He is the author of *Micronesia: Trust Betrayed* and numerous contributions to professional and scholarly journals.

Herman W. Nickel is Ambassador-in-residence at Johns Hopkins University's School of Advanced International Studies. He served as U.S. Ambassador to the Republic of South Africa from 1982 to 1986. Previously, Mr. Nickel was, for twenty years, a correspondent for Time-Life News Service reporting from Johannesburg, Washington, and London. He was Bureau Chief in Bonn, Tokyo, and London. From 1978 to 1981 he was a member of the Board of Editors of *Fortune Magazine*. Since returning from South Africa, Mr. Nickel has written articles for *SAIS Review* and other journals.

The Right Honourable Lord Francis Pym served as a member of Parliament from 1961 to 1987. During his tenure he occupied many government and opposition positions including; Government Chief Whip and Parliamentary Secretary of Treasury, Opposition Spokesman for Agriculture, for House of Commons Affairs and Devolution, for Foreign and Commonwealth Affairs, Chancellor of Duchy of Lancaster and Leader of the House of Commons, and Lord President of the Council and Leader of the House of Commons. In the British Cabinet Lord Pym served as Secretary of State for Northern Ireland from 1973 to 1974, Secretary of State for Defense from 1979 to 1981, and Secretary of State for Foreign and Commonwealth Affairs from 1982 to 1983.

Gregory F. Treverton is Senior Fellow at the Council on Foreign Relations with responsibility for European and politico-military issues, and the Director of the European American Project. He has worked in the U.S. government on the staff of the first Senate Select Committee on Intelligence (the Church Committee) and as staff member for Western Europe on the National Security Council during the Carter Administration. He was Director of Studies at the International Institute for Strategic Studies in London, and, immediately before joining the Council, was for six years a faculty member of the John F. Kennedy School of Government at Harvard. He is the author of *The "Dollar Drain" and American Forces in Germany, Nuclear Weapons in Europe, Making the Alliance Work: The United States and Western Europe*, and, most recently, *Covert Action: The Limits of Intervention in the Postwar World*.

Max van der Stoel served as the Netherlands Permanent Representative to the United Nations from 1983 to 1986 and is presently a member of the Netherlands Council of State. Previously he held the position of Minister of Foreign Affairs from 1973 to 1977 and from 1981 to 1982. In addition, he has served in both the First and Second Chambers of the Netherlands Parliament and as State Secretary of Foreign Affairs. He is a former member of the Council of Europe, the Atlantic Association, the European Parliament, and the Executive Board of the Socialist International.

Europe, America and South Africa

Introduction:
Framing the Issues

Gregory F. Treverton

This book is not about southern or South Africa, but rather about European and American policy, and the prospects for trans-Atlantic strain or cooperation. Its authors depart from two shared conclusions: that dramatic change is unlikely to come soon to South Africa, and so Europe and America need to conceive of policy for the long term; and that South Africa is at the center of the region's agony and so cannot be addressed apart from its interconnections with its neighbors.

The goal of the book is to provide a sharp sense for the differences among the allies and their points of convergence, the opportunities and dangers they face as they confront the tragic tangle of issues in southern Africa. The chapters are personal, providing different national perspectives on the domestic—and thus alliance—politics of the range of issues at play. They are written by five distinguished statesmen, people whose politics differ but who have thought hard about South Africa, in and out of their national governments. This introduction can only provide an overview of their judgments, where they agree and where they do not.

The issues can be grouped in five clusters. First are assessments of the situation in South Africa and the prospects for change: are those judgments broadly shared across the Atlantic, or are there critical differences that underlie approaches to policy? Second, how different are the interests of the allies—economic, mineral and strategic? Third is the question of how much leverage the allies have, separately or together. That question runs in the first instance to sanctions but also raises the

Peter Vale, Research Professor and Director of the Institute of Social and Economic Research at Rhodes University, Grahamstown, South Africa, has enriched this introduction; more important, he has, as a friend and colleague, helped me understand the tangle of southern Africa. Only the desire not to implicate him in my judgments spares him identification as a co-author.

value of positive inducements. Fourth are the connections between South Africa and its neighbors.

A final theme runs through all the discussion: for all the allies, but perhaps especially for the United States, South Africa is emotive in domestic politics because of the special dimension of race. What will those politics mean for policy-making within the alliance?

The Politics of Stalemate

As a starting-point for those inside or outside South Africa attempting to influence its politics, the current situation presents a tragic paradox. On one hand, the pace of events seems to have accelerated. Yet on the other the government has set itself against dramatic change, and the black opposition cannot bring that government to its knees. The history of the last several years testifies to that stalemate. On that history, the authors of this book are agreed.

As recently as the beginning of 1986, there were high hopes on both sides of the Atlantic that South Africa's whites would enter into negotiations to share power with their black country-men. The Commonwealth-sponsored Eminent Persons Group (EPG) seemed near to bridging the divide between South African State President P.W. Botha and Nelson Mandela, the imprisoned leader of the long-banned African National Congress (ANC).

But in May 1986, these hopes were dashed when South Africa sent armed raids into three neighboring states and followed the raids, three weeks later, with the imposition of a nationwide State of Emergency. The Emergency remains in force, and the South African Defense Force (SADF) retains a strong interventionist stance in southern Africa. These events frame the strategy of the Botha government—toward South Africa's black community, toward white politics and toward the region—and so are the backdrop for the longer-term assessments of this book.

From the white government's perspective, the tough security policy toward the black community has yielded some political dividends. The State of Emergency aimed to reverse the setbacks the government suffered after the 1976 insurrection associated with the name "Soweto," when its efforts to control the domestic political agenda were systematically undercut by its opponents.

Widespread arrests of government opponents, particularly supporters of the United Democratic Front (UDF), have created a political vacuum in the country's urban black areas, and the government has used this space in an effort to undermine what Botha calls the "revolutionary climate." It has deployed an ambitious strategy of cooption, which borrows from the counter-revolutionary theorists of the 1960s and 1970s.[1] The strategy turns on the notion that investment in social infrastructure can eliminate the root causes of political upheaval by building a political partnership with such blacks as can be induced to participate.

Given the historical levels of economic and social deprivation in South Africa, it is not surprising that this strategy has registered limited success. Millions of Rand have been poured into black urban areas, creating a sharp dilemma for black communities: improvements in the quality of local life derive from a government that itself enjoys scant legitimacy.

The government has tried various forms of partnership, but all have maintained two overriding principles: "group" interests are defined along racial lines, and ultimate power will remain in white hands. At the local level, a system of "management committees" and "town councils" comprise representatives of these various "group" interests. Recently constituted "regional services councils" bring black local authorities together with white municipalities in what the government claims is "multiracial" local government, and there is a proposal for black-elected regional councils to represent blacks who do not live in the so-called homelands. Black representation on provincial executives adds to the facade of multiracialism.

At the national level, the coloured and Indian communities participate in a tricameral legislature with whites, and the government has floated a number of proposals for somehow involving blacks in a "national council." In April 1988 Botha suggested a national forum for debating constitutional issues, plus the possible inclusion of blacks in both a downgraded President's Council and the nation's electoral college.

The ruling National Party, aware of the need to be seen to be engaged in a process of dialogue, has portrayed these initiatives, at least abroad, as the beginning of "multiracial" government that betokens a willingness to "negotiate" with the black majority over the country's future—representation in the electoral college would for the first time give blacks a role in governing whites through the selection of the state president. At the same time, however, the determination to retain white power is clear: the restructuring of local government has been paralleled by an increasing hold on public life by the national security management system (NSMS), which has joined the smallest towns and hamlets in a white-controlled security network. Foreign Minister van der Stoel shares the conclusion of the EPG report: the South African government's "quest is power-sharing, but without surrendering overall white control."

The NSMS system was established under the cover of the State of Emergency, and so provides the military and the police with a virtual *carte blanche* in dealing with troublesome black townships, all the more troublesome when black leaders who command some following are detained in prison. At the same time, the emphasis on security speaks to the fears of whites and thus reduces the risk to the government of being outflanked by the Conservative Party or other groups on its right.

The SADF stands at the apex of the NSMS through the State Security Council (SSC)—a body not accountable to the country's parliament or cabinet. Executive power in South Africa thus has become both extra-parliamentary and dominated by the SADF. This restructuring of government has weakened the prospects for change by drawing more and more whites into the bureaucratic-security mechanism, increasing the already enormous civil service and thus giving more whites a direct stake in the existing order.

Even aside from patronage, the South African government has demonstrated a remarkable capacity to mobilize support from the white population. Its pronouncements of the "total onslaught" of communism against South Africa, in which domestic turmoil results from outside instigation, often seem caricatures to outsiders. Yet they are broadly accepted by whites. A 1982 poll showed that four-fifths of all whites believed the government was not exaggerating the communist threat; among Afrikaans-speaking whites the percentage rose to 87.[2]

During the whites-only election of May 1987, the government played on these deep-seated fears. Security was the preoccupation of the white electorate, and the government took pains to portray the liberal opposition, the Progressive Federal Party (PFP), as "naive" and "soft" on communism. The outcome of the election underscored the drift to the right in white politics: the PFP was supplanted as the parliamentary opposition by the Conservative Party, an Afrikaner fundamentalist party to the right of the National Party.

In the run-up to the election, the prospect of defections to the left from the National Party raised hopes that negotiations might again return to the white political agenda. In the event, however, only one parliamentarian who had broken with the party over the slow pace of reform was returned to office. This outcome seemed to underscore a truism of white politics: the National Party fractures only to the right, not the left. Polls since the election have affirmed this proposition, finding that about a fifth of National Party supporters who before the election seemed willing to break away have since returned to the fold.

The gravitational pull of the party derives from the belief that significant change must come from within the party—a reaffirmation of the party's strong ethnic base that dates back to its formation. The pull is enhanced by the dominance of one man, President P.W. Botha, and his imprint on both governance and party unity. White politics is thus largely a struggle over the direction of the National Party.

Any belief in the white community, however, that life could return to "normal" in the wake of elections was belied by the re-emergence of civil unrest in the black townships around Pietermaritzburg, capital of Natal Province. That violence claimed the lives of some 90 blacks in January 1988 alone. There is no obvious way out of this cruel impasse. Blacks have a kind of veto over what remains of the government's "reform" agenda—each proposal for a "national council" founders on the government's inability to recruit blacks of stature to serve on it—but they cannot compel the government to adopt their own agenda. At the same time, however, local black leaders strain to control the "kids"—those young people who have no jobs and no hope of ever getting any, whose actions are born of desperation and whose trademark is the "necklace"—horrible death inflicted by burning tires around the bodies of victims.

If the impasse continues, it is hard to imagine that black opposition will not become even more violent—and more radical. The question for the chapters that follow is whether actions by the United States and the European nations can help produce real change in South Africa while averting that country's fall into the vortex of ever increasing violence.

Interests of the Allies

The second cluster of issues centers on European and American interests in southern Africa. In considering tangible interests, economic and mineral, Ambassador Nickel emphasizes the trans-Atlantic differences, and Lord Pym agrees. In the aggregate, American interests are relatively minor; those of France somewhat greater; those of the Federal Republic greater still, though hardly decisive. Only for Britain are tangible interests evidently significant. The total value of U.S. investments was about $2 billion at the end of 1984, down from a peak of 2.6 in 1981. Total lending by American banks doubled from 1978 to about $4.7 billion in 1984, but by 1986 more than half of the 105 largest U.S. banks had banned loans to the South African government, and 30 banks had banned all new loans.

By contrast, Prime Minister Thatcher has talked of some 120,000 British jobs depending on trade with South Africa. In 1985 British investment in South Africa accounted for 40 percent of all foreign investment in South Africa and for seven percent of total British investment overseas. Britain historically had been South Africa's main trading partner and source of investment. By 1980, however, South Africa accounted for only two percent of Britain's trade.[3] Yet given sluggish growth or, more recently, the relative paucity of jobs that growth created, lost jobs are not likely to be compensated by over-all growth.[4] South Africa's main trading partners are listed in Table 1, although the figures are only approximate because of South African government secrecy and the extent to which trade is routed through third countries (like Israel), then repackaged for its ultimate destination:

Table 1: Shares of South African Trade, 1984

	percent of South Africa's exports	percent of South Africa's imports
United States	8.4	15.9
Japan	7.7	12.9
Switzerland	6.8	
Britain	4.3	11.1
Federal Republic	3.9	15.7
Italy	2.5	3.5
Holland	2.4	
France	2.2	3.8
special categories (mainly gold for exports, oil and armaments for imports)	46.6	14.7

Source: International Monetary Fund, based on government statistics

For all the allies, save perhaps Britain, South Africa's main tangible significance is the rich array of minerals that lie beneath its soil, an interest all the authors recognize. Of these the most crucial is chromium, which the gods in their mirth distributed mostly in southern Africa and the Soviet Union. Table 2 lists South African production of key minerals and U.S. dependence on imports from that nation.

Table 2: Strategic Minerals in South Africa

	South Africa percentage of world production (1984)	South Africa percentage of world reserves (1984)	U.S. percentage reliance on South Africa (average, 1980-83)	U.S. percentage reliance on imports (average, 1982-4)
Chromium	27	83.6	55	82
Manganese	11	70.6	39	99
Platinum group	42	80.8	49	91
Vanadium	30	47.1	44	41

Source: U.S. Department of Commerce, "Report of Interagency Materials and Minerals Field Study to the Republic of South Africa, June 11, 1985

For the European nations, reliance on vital mineral imports, particularly from South Africa, is even greater than for the United States, hence they are even more vulnerable to disruptions.

Chromium has some substitutes for some uses, although not for the superalloys that are used in aircraft and nuclear-power systems. Manganese, unlike chromium, does not have substitutes, but does have other sources—Australia, Gabon and, eventually perhaps, seabed nodules. Substitutes for platinum are available, albeit at higher cost and lesser quality, while the United States itself is a major producer of vanadium.

In these circumstances, the only scenario of real concern would be a joint embargo of chromium exports by the three major producers—the Soviet Union, Zimbabwe and South Africa. That seems improbable; even if it occurred, its damage could be limited by stockpiling. Moreover, the Europeans and Americans writing in this book concur that concern over minerals does not point to any particular set of policies toward either the current or a future South African government. As Nickel puts it: ". . . any South African government of whatever complexion will have an overriding interest in selling minerals . . . . Thus there is little merit to the converging arguments from the far right and far left that the West should do the bidding of either present or future South African leaders."

The book's authors also agree in downplaying another stake that is sometimes thought to be of strategic importance—the Cape sea route.[5] In that view they have the company of the U.S. Secretary of State's 1987 advisory panel on South Africa.[6] It always was hard to imagine exactly how the Cape route mattered in connection with developments inside South Africa.[7] The Cape route is not a choke point but rather a thousand-mile span of ocean. If the Soviet Union decided to interfere with Western shipping—an act of war, after all—or even to disrupt that shipping less visibly through the actions of proxies, it would have more convenient places in which to do so, the Persian Gulf being an example.

How Much Leverage

If the United States and Europe have modest concrete stakes in southern Africa, so, too, their influence seems modest. On that the authors also agree. Their view contrasts with the public discussion of the issue, particularly in the United States, which often implies that the right combination of external carrots and sticks might induce real change in South Africa. If, then, that change does not occur, it must be because Europe and America (and Japan) do not wish it. For the authors, this view, understandable enough, is wishful thinking for those who hold it, both inside and outside South Africa.

The chapters underscore the considerable strengths of South Africa's economic position, all the more since the government has been confronting the prospect of sanctions for a generation. The economy is an open one; exports and imports total 60 percent of the country's GNP. However, 55 percent of exports by value are gold, platinum and diamonds—especially the former, which accounts for about half. Those are high-value, low-bulk commodities that would be difficult to keep from reaching markets.

South Africa's most critical imports are oil, capital goods and technology. If oil prices remain relatively low, South Africa no doubt would find no shortage of countries willing to sell it oil. With South Africa's long seacoast and trade connections elsewhere in Africa, it would be able to get that oil home, although the circuitous routes and subterfuge required would increase the effective price. Moreover, years of quiet stockpiling combined with Sasol oil-from-coal plants have given the country perhaps a decade's oil supply in hand.[8]

Nor is the country much vulnerable to departures by foreign companies—disinvestment—at least in the short run. The foreign companies' operating facilities in South Africa remain, so disinvestment only creates short-run bargains for South African capitalists. Indeed, when the British bank, Barclays, sold its stake in its South African affiliate in 1986, the local companies that bought it advertised that "the bank has come home." In the three years prior to 1984, 45 American companies left or sold out in South Africa, while 11 began new investments. Fifteen more left by August 1985. Most that left, like Pan-American Airways, did so because they were unprofitable. And many—Coca-Cola and Pepsico, for instance—sold out to local entrepreneurs.[9]

On the other hand, with or without government policies, South Africa will be subjected to limits on its foreign economic interactions. Foreign firms will make their own decisions about investments in South Africa; those assessments will be "economic," but they will include calculations of the country's political future. The actions by American banks in the summer of 1985 still overshadow any other sanctions in their economic effect on South Africa.[10] In the middle of the violence in South Africa, Chase Manhattan announced that it would not roll over $400 million in short-term loans. Other American banks followed suit and refused to roll over about $1 billion in short-term loans. A financial crisis in South Africa ensued.

Divestment campaigns have the effect of making foreign companies wary of the bad publicity and so make them reluctant to make large new investments in South Africa. When large units of government, like California or New York City, have threatened to stop doing business with, or divest their pension funds of, companies with subsidiaries in South Africa, corporate giants like IBM have had to compare their large stakes in those units with their small business in South Africa. Thus, there will be virtually no new foreign investment in South Africa whatever the national policies of the allies.

The Question of Sanctions

If, however this book's authors concur in their assessment of South Africa's limited vulnerability, they disagree over the implications of that assessment for policy. However, while the difference in actual policy toward sanctions separates the United States from the European nations, as Table 3 indicates, the analytic lines in this book are not so clear. The question divides the European and American authors nearly as much as it separates the two groups. All agree, however, that the debate in the West has been both too simplistic and too preoccupied with sanctions. Sanctions are *an* issue but not *the* issue.

Ambassador Nickel makes the strongest case against sanctions, although he would stop short of dismantling sanctions already on the books, for to do so would be to reward the South African government for "behavior that has become even worse than it was at the time the original sanctions were imposed." For him, sanctions have failed in every dimension. He echoes much of the literature on sanctions in arguing that they are flawed in concept: ". . . in most circumstances, the suggestion that policies designed to shrink the economic pie will facilitate the peaceful resolution of sociopolitical conflict would be dismissed as mad."

And, indeed, since sanctions were imposed, the situation in South Africa has become worse, not better, even if sanctions do not deserve all or even most of the blame. Reform is in tatters, as whites appear to have retreated to the proverbial laager. "No politician . . . likes to be seen as surrendering to foreign pressure, least of all Afrikaner politicians." Moreover, sanctions have driven the business community and the government closer together, not further apart.

For Nickel, the sad irony is that sanctions have diminished the influence of the West in general and the United States in particular, not enhanced it. When any reform is dismissed in the U.S. Congress as cosmetic, white South African leaders have calculated that "if it took political suicide to stave off sanctions, sanctions were the lesser evil." And the more Western demands escalated, the more tempting it was to "call the bluff."

Table 3: Current EC and U.S. Sanctions against South Africa[a]

	EC	U.S.
Import Bans		
Ammunition, Arms & Military Vehicles	Yes	Yes
Agricultural products & Food	No	Yes
Coal	No	Yes
Pig Iron and Steel	Yes	Yes
Textiles	No	Yes
Uranium Ore	No	Yes
Ban on Landing rights for South African aircraft	No	Yes
Export Bans		
Computer goods and services to police and military	Yes[b]	Yes
Oil	Yes[b]	Yes
Technical support and services to civilian and military nuclear industries	Yes[b, c]	Yes
Ban on new investment in South Africa	Yes	Yes
Ban on Export Support i.e., export credits and promotion	No	Yes

a) This table is not a complete listing of the sanctions in place, rather it is meant to highlight some of the more important differences between the sanctions policies of the United States and the EC.

b) Does not include exports to South African controlled Namibia.

c) EC ban prohibits "new collaboration in the nuclear sector."

Source: *The Sanctions Handbook*, Penguin Books, London, 1987

The opposite case on sanctions is argued by Ambassador McHenry and Foreign Minister van der Stoel. McHenry notes that Europeans tend to be opposed to sanctions in principle, against the Soviet Union as well as South Africa. Yet "even the strongest opponents of sanctions tend to support them under extreme provocation." Both men concede that economic sanctions, especially limited ones, hardly can be decisive in the short run. McHenry, in particular, laments that the European states did not follow the U.S. lead in the Comprehensive Anti-Apartheid Act of 1986 and that the Reagan Administration, which opposed the Act, did not implement its provision calling for an effort to bring American allies into agreement.

Even if far-reaching economic sanctions do not seem politically possible and would not bring the South African order down quickly in any event, sanctions can play a role in long-term policy. In McHenry's words: "Sanctions alone did not lead the Rhodesian government to the negotiating table. But sanctions weakened Rhodesia, causing it to open inefficient industries; to pay middle men exorbitant profits for imports while receiving low payments for exports; and to risk serious shortages of spare parts."

Foreign Minister Cheysson regards economic sanctions as morally imperative even if practically ineffective, but he would oppose restrictions on contacts between South Africans—black and white—and the rest of the world. By contrast, van der Stoel makes a strong argument for political and psychological sanctions, especially those, like boycotts on sports contacts or on landing rights, that have primary effect on whites—testimony that those whites "are entering into a confrontation with the Western world to which they want so much to belong." He would accompany these sticks with carrots—promises of aid, given at the highest level, provided white South Africa embarked on radical reform.

McHenry and van der Stoel take seriously the argument that sanctions hurt black South Africans, perhaps more than whites—an argument made eloquently in South Africa by Helen Suzman and repeated by President Reagan and Prime Minister Thatcher. The harm is a fact, but many black leaders themselves have called for sanctions, Bishop Desmond Tutu most prominent among them. Moreover, this argument against sanctions would have force only if there were an alternative, something other than violence that showed promise of bringing real change to South Africa. To the proposition that economic growth is the way to real reform in South Africa, McHenry answers that if growth has in the past improved the lot of black South Africans, "it has made no dent on the item of dispute: political power."

All the authors favor continued efforts, both public and private, to support anti-apartheid groups and promote black education and social programs, both inside and outside South Africa. The total of such assistance to anti-apartheid and human rights groups came to some $250 million in 1987. There is the risk that South Africa will retaliate against such assistance—that it will not let the West replace "constructive engagement" with "selective engagement"—as it already has threatened. That threat is real even if it is diminished by South Africa's awareness that assistance denied would be diverted to groups outside South Africa over which Pretoria has even less control.

The Regional Connection

The discussion of sanctions highlights the fourth cluster of issues—connections between South Africa and its neighbors. Those neighbors are deeply dependent on trade routes through South Africa. Sanctions, which to be effective would have to be applied to those neighbors as well, could make that dependence crippling, especially if South Africa retaliated against them. The degrees of dependence vary from year to year—and depend on the success of South African-backed rebels in closing down rail lines in Angola and Mozambique—but something like 50 to 60 percent of trade by Malawi, Zambia and Zimbabwe transits South Africa, and for Botswana, Lesotho and Swaziland the percentages are in the 80 to 100 percent range.

Like it or not, South Africa is the hub of the region. For several of the authors, Nickel in particular, this vulnerability of South Africa's neighbors is an argument against sanctions. Neighboring states should not be compelled to suffer the effects of policies they have been unwilling to implement on their own.

If sanctions made South Africa more dependent on neighbors as blockade-runners and so it became reluctant to retaliate against them, that would only underscore the leakiness of sanctions.

All the chapters evoke the vulnerability of South Africa's neighbors—to sanctions, armed raiders or South African attacks on its political opponents. Despite peace agreements and optimistic forecasts, violence in southern Africa has been increasing. So, too, South African destabilization has continued: to that proposition, the May 1986 raids and less dramatic successors are testimony. Earlier in 1986, in January, South Africa engineered a relatively bloodless coup in Lesotho against an autocratic leader who had been reluctant to expel ANC leaders and who had the audacity to establish diplomatic relations with the Soviet Union and several of its allies. Within two weeks, a railroad blockade brought the economy to a standstill and resulted in a change of government.

Over the past few years, the allies have been moving in different directions over policy toward the southern African region, a difference outlined in this book's chapters. Pym and van der Stoel are sharply critical of American policy; as Pym puts it, that policy has developed so many contradictions— "between the strongly anti-apartheid position. . . and the lack of convincing support for the Front Line States;. . . and between the United States offering itself as an honest broker on Cuban troop withdrawal [from Angola] while simultaneously providing military assistance to UNITA"—as to "generate a credibility gap for the United States in southern Africa."

American policy during the Reagan Administration, "constructive engagement," so called, sought to "underpromise and overdeliver."[11] Accordingly, the United States would reverse the (relatively minor) sanctions enacted by the Carter Administration and would avoid overt pressure on South Africa, which had only seemed to promise more to black South Africans than the United States could deliver.

Yet if the means of constructive engagement were low-key, the objectives were ambitious: if the United States could broker a deal in Namibia along the lines of United Nations Resolution 435, which called for a cease-fire and internationally-supervised elections, then it might induce the Cubans to pull out of Angola and move Jonas Savimbi and his UNITA (Union for the Total Independence of Angola) forces into a national unity government with the Marxist MPLA (Popular Movement for the Liberation of Angola) that governed the country; and at the same time build stability in Zimbabwe and Mozambique, including early mention of economic aid and even military assistance. Thus, it might lay the basis for reform in South Africa. As Secretary of State George Shultz said in April 1985: "a white government that no longer sees itself as besieged from outside its borders will be better able to take the steps it must to reform its own society."[12]

Under the policy of constructive engagement, three neighboring states had been lured into making agreements with South Africa, agreements that were hailed as a dramatic break in previous regional relations. Also, early in 1984 South Africa concluded a cease-fire with Angola and, more striking still, a mutual nonaggression pact with Mozambique (the Nkomati accord); at the same time it was revealed that a similar agreement had been concluded with Swaziland in 1982. By 1985, however, constructive engagement was in tatters. So judged the U.S. Secretary of State's Advisory Panel in 1987.

Under the Nkomati accord, Mozambique was to crack down on ANC guerrillas operating into South Africa, while South Africa agreed to cease support for RENAMO (the Mozambican National Resistance Movement, also known as MNR). While there was a brief decline in ANC attacks staged from Mozambique against South Africa in 1984, RENAMO actions in Mozambique actually increased after the agreement, and it became public that covert South African support for the shadowy movement continued into 1985. (ANC actions in South Africa also increased in 1985 and 1986 but few incidents were as damaging or spectacular as those in 1981-84.) In 1988, Pretoria restricted specific actions of RENAMO in order to protect hydro-electric plants vital to South Africa as well as Mozambique. There is no evidence to suggest, however, that South Africa has ended its overall support for RENAMO.

In the United States, pressure from the right converted the removal of Cubans from Angola from a hoped-for consequence of a Namibia settlement to an element of it, thus putting the U.S. into tacit alliance with Pretoria on that question and taking the heat off South Africa to cut a deal.

In early 1988 Cuba joined the U.S.-mediated talks and declared itself willing to set a date for the withdrawal of all its forces. Yet if there was a deal at all, it seemed likely to be an Angola-only deal; the high hopes of the late 1970s over Namibia had given way to the gnawing prospect that Namibian independence might have to be the product, not the precursor to real change inside South Africa.

Long before 1988, moreover, Congress had prevented the Administration from delivering on some of its undertakings toward Mozambique, and the Reagan Administration persuaded Congress to mix anti-apartheid policy in South Africa with anti-communism in Angola, through the resumption in 1986 of covert support to Jonas Savimbi's UNITA. Indeed, as van der Stoel notes, while the Europeans were bringing Angola into the Lomé convention, the United States was still trying to isolate it by withholding diplomatic relations.

Whatever their views on sanctions, all the authors favor Western efforts to diminish southern Africa's dependence on South Africa. The Europeans regret that the sanctions mandated by the U.S. Congress on South Africa have not been accompanied by aid for South Africa's neighbors. For their part, some of the allies have worked to develop links to the Front Line States—through financing the redevelopment of the Beira corridor linking Zimbabwe with Mozambican ports or even providing some training to army units protecting those transit facilities. Britain, for instance, provided well over one billion dollars in assistance to those states during the period from 1980 to 1987, and its military training teams have been in Zimbabwe since 1980.

Politics and Policy

Most foreign policy issues are dominated by their domestic face, but the fact that Americans can scarcely help viewing southern

Africa through the prism of their own unfinished racial agenda
seems to make that domestic political face especially prominent.
Europeans, like Pym, underscore that difference in perspective—
"events in South Africa fuel domestic pressures in the United
States"—and an American, Nickel, agrees. Another American,
McHenry, does not disagree that the politics of the issue are
different, but he emphasizes broader American traditions, not
just the specific politics of race. He also notes other differences:
the absence of American "kith and kin" ties to white South
Africa of the sort Britain has; the American federal structure that
all but lets states and localities run their own South African
policies; parliamentary traditions in Europe that still insulate
foreign policy from domestic pressures, even if that difference
often is overstated; and the traditional European Realpolitik that
accords less attention to the internal practices of foreign states.

For both the Europeans and Americans writing in this book,
the imperative is for the allies to act together. South Africa
enjoys decided advantages over its opponents; disunity among
the allies lets it play on those advantages. If the United States
and Europe have little enough influence even when united, they
have even less when divided. This book stakes out considerable
common ground: programs to help black South Africans and to
reduce the dependence of the Front Line States on South Africa,
coupled with contacts with a range of opposition groups,
including the ANC, with which the Reagan Administration
began contacts.

Yet differences remain. They are most visible, if perhaps not
most important, over sanctions. Electoral seasons in the United
States, like that of 1988, make this trans-Atlantic divide more
salient. Sanctions rise on the agenda, with Democratic politicians
competing to see who can be more against apartheid, and
Republicans not far behind. As in 1986, South Africa's own
actions make another round of sanctions inevitable in any case.
Domestic politics makes the eventual result unpredictable. Also
as in 1986, domestic politics makes the eventual outcome
unpredictable. Then, the Kennedy-Gray sanctions bill, introduced in May and produced before the South African raids into
its neighboring states, was nearly overtaken in the wake of the

the South African emergency. In a voice vote, the House of Representatives approved a much tougher substitute bill, one that would have compelled complete disinvestment in 180 days, banned all trade with South Africa, and ended South African landing rights in the United States. The eventual bill, passed over President Reagan's veto, was along the lines of the Kennedy-Gray proposal, but the episode indicated just how vulnerable American policy could be to the vagaries of the political season.

If the allies cannot manage a united policy, how serious will that be for their alliance? On that score, too, the authors seem agreed, an agreement more negative than positive. NATO will not split up over South Africa—the Commonwealth has survived despite greater pressure. South Africa will be a source of strain in the alliance, but it will not be of the highest priority for any of the allies. In McHenry's words, "although the situation in South Africa is one of extraordinary cruelty, it is unlikely to have an incendiary effect on international peace and security." If disunity will not risk an alliance crisis, it will forfeit an opportunity to play a positive role in addressing that cruelty. It will not be a disaster for the alliance, but it will be a shame for the international community.

Notes

1. For example, John J. McCuen, *The Art of Counter-revolutionary War: The Struggle of Counter-insurgency*, (London: Faber and Faber, 1966); or Ted Gurr, Why Men Rebel, (Princeton: Princeton University Press, 1970).
2. See Deon Geldenhuys, *What Do We Think? A Survey of White Opinion on Foreign Policy Issues*, (Braamfontein: South African Institute of International Affairs, November 1982).
3. James Barber, *The Uneasy Relationship: Britain and South Africa*, (London: Heinemann. 1983), p. 31.
4. This is the conclusion of the best study on the subject, that by Peter C.J. Vale, *The Atlantic Nations and South Africa: Economic Constraints and Community Fracture*, unpublished dissertation, University of Leicester, 1980. Though his data are now somewhat dated, his conclusion are still apposite.

5. For a recent exposition of this view, now distinctly in the minority, see Robert J. Hanks, *Southern Africa and Western Security*, (Cambridge, MA: Institute for Foreign Policy Analysis, August 1983,) especially pp. 2-15.
6. US Secretary of State's Advisory Panel Report, Department of State, January 1987.
7. See Robert B. Shepard, "South Africa: The Case for Disengagement," *The National Interest*, (Winter 1986), pp. 52-3.
8. John D. Battersby, "South Africa: Sanctions," *Africa Report*, (January-February 1987), p. 7.
9. As reported in *Finance Times* (South Africa), August 22-28, 1985, pp. 507-08.
10. *Sunday Times* (Johannesburg), June 15, 1986.
11. See Chester A. Crocker, "South Africa: Strategy for Change," *Foreign Affairs*, (Winter 1980/81), pp. 323-51.
12. Address before the National Press Club, quoted in Herbert Howe, "United States Policy in Southern Africa," *Current History*, (May 1986), p. 206.

Strains among Friends: Coordinating Western Policy toward South Africa

The Right Honorable Lord Pym, PC, MC

Although the greatest threat to world peace today lies in the Middle East, the very different problems of South Africa and apartheid are potentially almost as intractable and dangerous— and of equally long standing. The countries of the West are all involved in their differing ways. Indeed the individual citizens of these countries are involved in so far as a large majority condemn apartheid and call for something to be done. The Western governments are honorable in their intentions to bring about a peaceful end to the system but have been far from unanimous in what action to take. At times Western disarray has been evident and damaging. Without doubt the South African question causes enormous strains even among friends. Why is apartheid so difficult to deal with? What should be done?

The Historical Origins of Different Western Perceptions

The starting point of any answer must be the historical background. Africa was the colonial continent par excellence. At the full height of the colonial period the whole continent was someone's colony (or equivalent)—except for just three independent sovereign states: South Africa, Liberia, and Ethiopia. The British, French, Dutch, Portuguese, Germans, Spanish, and Belgians had forged strong links with their various colonies. The development of the whole continent was inspired and directed by Europeans, and today the legacy can be seen in the various languages, traditions, cultures, boundaries and economic relationships of the fifty or more independent countries of Africa.

The British and the Dutch were involved in South Africa earlier and more deeply than many of their fellow Europeans elsewhere in the continent. The Dutch established themselves at the Cape more than three centuries ago—long enough to become a proud new people, the Afrikaners, with a new language, Afrikaans, in which their identity is emotionally bound up. The British came on the scene a hundred years later and, over a period of one hundred and fifty years after that, they and the Afrikaners vied for control of the southern end of Africa. This rivalry culminated in the Boer Wars.

I use the plural in deference to the Afrikaners who see their struggle with the British as a series of engagements beginning with their defeat of the British at the battle of Majuba Hill in 1881, which led to the virtual independence of the republics of the Transvaal and the Orange Free State. Twenty years after this First War of Independence came what we call the Boer War— and what the Afrikaners call the Second National War of Independence. After prolonged and bitter fighting the British prevailed, but their efforts to establish a union in which British and Afrikaners would work together foundered on the opposition of the National Party and its secret arm, the Broederbond, which sought to unite Afrikanerdom against the British. By 1948 the opposition had sufficiently achieved this aim to be able to bring to bear the numerical superiority of the Afrikaners to win the general election that year.

This historical sketch shows that we the British are more intimately linked to South Africa than any other European power. The Dutch were assimilated into the Afrikaners with their own distinct identity. The British retained their mother tongue in South Africa with all that that implies. Britain has supplied a steady flow of immigrants. Large numbers of South Africans fought with us in the two world wars. We have huge investments in South Africa and there are well nigh inextricable links between our economy and the South African economy. Indeed, there may well be up to one million people in South Africa who have a claim to a British passport. For better or worse the British are involved.

Powerless after 1948, the British looked on as the Afrikaners set about establishing a legally structured racist system in South Africa—at just the time when everywhere else in the postwar world the emphasis was on independence rather than colonialism, racial integration and equality rather than discrimination. It was from a thoroughly informed position that Harold Macmillan made his far-sighted "Wind of Change" speech in the South African Parliament in 1961. Sharpeville in 1960 had already focused the world's and United Nations' attention on South Africa, and it has stayed there ever since. We are all depressingly familiar with the repetitive sequence of events since then. The frustration of the blacks has led to calls for mandatory economic sanctions that have been rejected by some Western countries as ineffective and counterproductive. Arguments by Western countries that they can use their links to influence change in the direction of reform have been made to look, however unjustly, like a cynical cloak for the preservation of Western commercial interests.

While there is much common ground among the European members of the Western alliance, there have also been differences of policy toward South Africa and apartheid. In the European Community, the desire for political consensus is made difficult by the different interests of each member. The issue of human rights is a live one among European electorates, who want action but dislike violence. They look for ways to give South African blacks their rights but without bloodshed. Sanctions are an easy option only in so far as a country's interests pose no conflict.

Thus, Britain and the Federal Republic have similar commercial interests and follow similar policies. The French were prepared to sell advanced modern weapons to South Africa long after other members of the Western alliance had ceased to do so. The main interest of the four EC countries in the southern tier may prove to be their communities in South Africa: there are about half a million Portuguese and 150,000 Greeks in South Africa. The Nordics have always taken a more "moral" and openly pro-black attitude—which is easier for them since they have little commercial interest at stake. The Dutch have a special

position because of their historical and cultural involvement
with Afrikanerdom, though they do not claim any special
influence on that account. However, none of these differences
within Europe are likely to become very significant politically.

For Britain, the Commonwealth, with its large black populations that naturally feel passionately about South Africa, is also
a tug. The Commonwealth forms a strong sanctions lobby
because that seems the only way to apply pressure on the South
African government and express resentment on behalf of their
fellow blacks. Britain remains adamantly against mandatory
sanctions and argues this case regularly in the forums of both
the Commonwealth and the European Community.

The biggest difference, however, has been between Europe as
a whole and the United States. In marked contrast to the
European countries, the United States was hardly involved in
the colonial scramble for Africa. It was preoccupied with
pushing its own frontiers westward, creating in the process the
most powerful nation on earth. Consequently, it had little
interest in, or resources for, excursions into Africa, though there
was some commerce and considerable missionary activity. Even
today, however, less than 1 percent of American trade is with
South Africa. It was not until the mid–1970s that the United
States really woke up to the fact that there were important issues
of human rights and East-West relations at stake in central and
southern Africa.

These different histories on each side of the Atlantic give rise
to very different perspectives on the South African problem.
Everyone detests apartheid, but the emotional and passionate
reaction to it by black people everywhere puts it into a category
all of its own for them. This is where the one significant
involvement of Americans with Africa—the slave trade—plays a
part, for its black minority is numerically and politically
important. In the United States the problem of apartheid is a
commentary on, and a reflection of, the nation's own racial
problems. Apartheid evokes memories of the Civil War and of
the civil rights campaigns of the 1960s and 1970s. In the
American style the lobbying of Congress by blacks on behalf of
their fellow blacks in South Africa applies heavy pressure for

effective action. Such pressures have evoked differences between Congress and the administration and between the two political parties.

This trans-Atlantic difference will be magnified by domestic politics, which increasingly influences foreign policy, an influence scarcely admitted by politicians. In the technological age this influence has grown massively. Television provides new opportunities for minorities and special interests to advertise demands that cannot always be resisted, and indeed should not be. In the United States, presidential primaries and congressional elections are bound to increase the power of special-interest lobbies. Lobbying is a wholly legitimate and democratic activity, but its demands are not necessarily right or appropriate. Indeed, lobbying could make a situation worse. So the politician seeking election has to strike a balance between what he believes to be the best policy in a particular matter and what his electorate will support.

The pressures for strong action against South Africa will prove severe, especially in the United States. It is argued, for instance by Ambassador McHenry in his chapter, that the engine of this campaign is not domestic political pressure in the United States but events in South Africa itself. Yet the truth seems slightly different: events in South Africa fuel domestic pressures in the United States. The one is the consequence of the other, as was the case with the Comprehensive Anti-Apartheid Act. Events in South Africa and American racial problems are thus closely interconnected.

These domestic pressures exist alongside the U.S. concern to counter communism and promote free enterprise economies throughout southern Africa as elsewhere. Ideological and strategic concerns incline both Congress and the executive branch to see the problem in the global context of East-West rivalry. This clash of foreign policy concerns with domestic political pressures was reflected in the debate over "constructive engagement." Not well received in the region or by some traditional friends in the West, the policy was also divisive within the Reagan Administration as well as between Congress and the Administration. While the Administration opposed tighter economic sanctions,

Congress imposed them, an action that went a long way to restoring the black community's faith in the ideals of American justice. Congressional sanctions reinforced the separate but parallel phenomenon of disinvestment by U.S. companies, while the Administration continued to support a strong U.S. corporate presence as a "critical force for peaceful change" in South Africa.

There is also a contradiction on the one hand between the strong anti-apartheid position of the United States and the lack of convincing support for the Front Line States; and on the other between the United States offering itself as an honest broker on Cuban troop withdrawal while simultaneously providing military assistance to UNITA. To put it mildly, these contradictions generate a credibility gap for the United States in southern Africa and underline the need for clarity on aims.

Because of its racial dimension and higher political profile the South Africa issue requires much tougher and more forthright handling in the United States than in Europe. This is so even though U.S. economic and trade interests are proportionately much smaller. There can be no doubt whatever that internal pressures will have a powerful effect on policy-making in the United States, while no similar pressures exist in Europe. In Britain, for example, with its long involvement with South Africa, there is a variety of pressures, smaller in scale and some of them conflicting: on the one hand the moral abhorrence of apartheid, the historical responsibilities toward black South Africans, the obligations to neighboring Commonwealth and other states; and on the other hand the vested economic and trade interests. The balance of pressures is fine; the result is wide agreement in Britain that ending apartheid cannot be achieved without some cost.

Afrikaner Fears, Black Hopes

Inside South Africa, deep down many Afrikaners have a vision of an ideal society in which all South Africa's various racial components would cooperate happily together, the whites playing an acknowledged leading role because of their supposedly greater intellectual and admittedly larger material resources, which they would happily dedicate to the community as a whole. There is, or at least was, a strong paternalistic and religious dimension to this vision. Left to themselves, without outside interference, Afrikaners are confident that they could manage things to everyone's satisfaction. But they find that their motives are impugned, and that "their" blacks are alienated. The British can recognize the latter phenomenon, from their wide decolonization experience, as the self-assertion that is normal on the way to political maturity. But the Afrikaners put it down to malign outside influences, or communism. Black "self-assertion" touches the nerve of Afrikaners' anxiety over the black majority among whom they live.

Their worst nightmare is of violent uprising by the blacks against the whites. There have been glimpses of this nightmare—for example, during the Soweto uprising of 1976—and it is no accident that about that time a new commitment to reform arose, one in which P. W. Botha has played the lead.

The reform process focused first on what is essentially a secondary issue—a proposed new relationship among whites and coloureds and Asians. While the President's Council was at work on new constitutional structures in this regard, the South African government continued by administrative action the homelands policy by which all South African blacks would belong to one of ten "independent" states, and blacks from the homelands would enter South Africa as foreign migrant workers. By the early 1980s four homelands had become "independent" (Transkei, Bophuthatswana, Venda, and Ciskei), and moves were afoot to grant independence to a fifth (KwaNdebele). There was talk of giving QwaQua to Lesotho and KaNgwane to Swaziland. The consummation of the Homelands Policy seemed almost on the horizon, but then troubles blew up in KwaNdebele, and the steam seemed to go out of the homelands policy.

It had always been made clear that the blacks could not expect the same "power-sharing" being offered to the coloureds and Asians in the proposed tricameral parliament, but the actual establishment of the parliament highlighted the inferior political position of the blacks. Intense black frustration was articulated by the United Democratic Front (UDF), a body set up in 1983 with radical aims but nonviolent methods. Black discontent was made manifest in extensive violence and a mass stay-away from work. An increasing number of arrests were made, as trouble broke out in township after township. Local authority virtually collapsed in many areas. Political views became more extreme. The government imposed a State of Emergency in July 1985, initially in 36 districts and then extended. During the first six months of this regime more than 7,000 people were detained without trial, over 3,600 of them under existing security legislation. Subsequently further restrictions were placed on the media, the conduct of funerals, and the movements of people in prescribed areas. The State of Emergency was lifted for three months in 1986 and then reimposed nationwide with further limits. There have been stringent new controls on the media.

As a result, although the government has carried through reforms it believes to be significant, the position of the blacks remains one of fundamentally inferior political rights. The reforms do alleviate some deeply resented controls and improve security of tenure for urban residence and employment, but little has been done for the larger number of rural blacks, especially in the homelands. Segregation in housing, schools, and hospitals is still enforced despite some improvements. The Population Registration Act continues to identify people for purposes of implementing discriminatory legislation. Living conditions for ordinary blacks are often appalling. High unemployment, child malnutrition, and gross overcrowding are widespread. Forced removals continue despite ministerial assurances to the contrary.

In this highly charged atmosphere, President Botha called a whites-only election on May 6, 1987, fought largely on the issues of security and external interference. The purpose of the election was to secure the support of the majority of white South Africans for the government's policy. There was very little mention of reform or concessions and much more of discipline and rigor. The result showed a clear shift to the right in white politics and gave P. W. Botha the sort of mandate that he wanted on security. It was in this context that the South African government announced that blacks would have the right to elect some representatives to a new National Council that will make recommendations on a new constitution in which all South Africans could participate in the processes of government. Few believe that this heralds any new arrangement under which blacks are to have any real power, and this remains true in spite of Botha's recent tackling of the right-wing whites.

In this environment of escalating black resentment, it is worth pausing over the oldest existing black nationalist movement anywhere, the African National Congress (ANC). Formed in 1912, the ANC quickly gathered support because of the Native Land Act of the following year. It paid great attention to the due processes of the law, none of which proved effective. It was not until 1940 that the ANC began to turn into a mass movement. In 1945 it adopted a list of "African claims" that included calls for universal suffrage, equal opportunities, the repeal of the pass laws, and the ending of racial discrimination—to no avail. In 1949 a number of activist members of the Youth League were elected to the ANC executive in place of more moderate members. They included Nelson Mandela, Oliver Tambo, and Walter Sisulu. At times the ANC worked closely with organizations like the Coloured People's Organization and the South African Indian Congress. The activities of these bodies were met with mounting repression, and after Sharpeville the ANC was banned. Its leaders then opted for a sabotage campaign against government targets, but one that avoided civilian casualties. The leaders were arrested in July 1963, and at the end of the the "Rivonia Trial" in June 1964, Mandela, Sisulu, and others were sentenced to life imprisonment.

After Soweto, the ANC stepped up this sabotage campaign to include some spectacular attacks on military and economic targets, such as the SASOL oil-from-coal installation in June 1980 and the Koeberg nuclear power station in December 1982. For its part, the UDF sought to mobilize resistance inside South Africa by all races on a national scale to the proposed tricameral parliament. Calls to boycott the vote resulted in less than 18 percent of the eligible coloured population casting ballots. It can be taken for granted that the ANC will oppose the South African government's plans for a new National Council with some elected black representation.

This outline of events throws into relief the current reality of South Africa. The Afrikaners won the fight to decide which white power was to be dominant in South Africa, but the Boer Wars did not decide and did not even address the question whether the whites or the more numerous blacks would be dominant in the long term. With superior weapons and technology, the whites have remained in decisive dominance so far, and it would be misleading to assume the quick erosion of white power: Afrikaner determination should never be underestimated. But ever since 1912 the blacks have been gathering their strength to mount an effective challenge to the whites. While they are not united, no credible black leader is likely to emerge who could persuade a majority of blacks to agree to any plans devised by the present South African government. The ultimate outcome of the struggle is no longer in doubt. By sheer weight of numbers and by growing expertise, the blacks are in the end bound to achieve their rightful position in their own country. The only question is how this will come about.

The prospects for a negotiated settlement are bleak because the crux of the matter remains what it always has been: the Afrikaners are prepared to be flexible but have not so far shown any sign of willingness to compromise on ultimate white control, while the blacks regard themselves as entitled to the power that derives from their overwhelming preponderance of numbers. It is very difficult to imagine the Afrikaners giving way in a negotiation; doing so would be quite against their character. The complete failure of the initiative of the Commonwealth Eminent Persons Group and of the visits to South Africa made in 1986 by Sir Geoffrey Howe on behalf of the European Community demonstrate the problems. With some shining exceptions, the Afrikaner attitude continues to be negative. The danger is that the laager will be reinforced and that, in circumstances presently impossible to foresee and at a time impossible to predict, an all-out confrontation will come.

The only hope seems to be that before that final agony the Afrikaners might come to see defeat as inevitable and concede at the last moment. This possibility does not enter their thinking at present: things have gone well for them in the past year. But in whatever timescale, it is vital that the white South Africans come to their senses before disaster strikes. Indeed, unless they do so disaster seems inevitable. Some of them may like to hope that the West will rally round to save them, but there is no question of that, and the sooner that is understood the more realistic will be their own perspective.

The Regional Dimension

As the alliance nations consider policy, they have to reckon with the fact that South Africa is the overwhelmingly dominant economic and military power in the region. South Africa is the chief trading partner of Botswana, Lesotho, and Swaziland (the BLS countries), which together with South Africa form the Southern African Customs Union (SACU). Revenues from this source are of major importance to the BLS countries. Botswana is highly dependent on South African transport links and 85 percent of its imports originate in South Africa. Lesotho is the country most closely tied to South Africa because of its geographical position and lack of natural resources. Remittances from 115,000 migrant workers account for no less than half of its GNP, and it is dependent upon South Africa for electricity and transport as well as investment. In Swaziland, 66 percent of recurrent government revenue comes from SACU, and 4 percent of the work force is employed by South Africa. South Africa provides 85 percent of Swazi imports and absorbs 30 percent of its exports.

So, too, the Front Line States are heavily dependent on South Africa. Until quite recently much of Zambia's rail freight passed through South Africa, including vital copper exports that provide a large percentage of its foreign earnings. South Africa is Zimbabwe's biggest trading partner and retains substantial investments there. Disruption to Mozambique's transport system has obliged Zimbabwe to divert up to 80 percent of its foreign trade through South Africa. In the case of Mozambique, South Africa provides 60 percent of Maputo's electricity and 43 percent of the port's throughput, and migrant workers in South Africa are estimated at around 50,000. Malawi is also dependent on South Africa, which supplies 36 percent of its imports and

whose transport system carries about half its exports. Angola is
the country least connected with South Africa, but there are still
economic links.

Militarily, South Africa's forces are alert, experienced, re-
sourceful, and well equipped. In Angola, South Africa has for
years mounted offensive operations in support of UNITA
requiring coordinated action by infantry, artillery, and aircraft.
Commando raids have been made on neighboring states. Defen-
sive and offensive guerrilla warfare has been organized in
Namibia and Angola against SWAPO. In addition, South
African forces have wide experience in dealing with riots and
civil disorder.

The South African concept of the "total onslaught" has
conditioned its citizens to regard their new black neighbors as
hostile. South Africans therefore see it to be in their interest that
their neighbors should be economically dependent and internally weak, thus lacking the economic freedom of action and the
military strength to constitute any threat to South Africa itself.
At the same time, South Africans are continually nervous about
the terrorism and sabotage carried out in South Africa from
bases in South Africa's black neighbors. Whenever the ANC can
be blamed for any outrage in South Africa, retribution follows,
regardless of the political or other consequences accompanying
an invasion of the sovereignty of a neighboring country. It is
said that the South African Defense Forces do not have enough
troops to guard the long frontier. They can therefore only
operate against the ANC or "terrorists" by attacking them where
they can be found; in the neighboring countries.

In theory at least, South African support for RENAMO in
Mozambique came to an end with the signature of the Nkomati
Accord in 1984. It is however widely believed that South Africa
continues to assist RENAMO in its outrageous attacks on
Mozambique. Mozambique is very short of resources, yet
struggling to survive. To undermine those efforts is cruel, to say
the least. The South Africans also apply economic pressures
from time to time. For example, South Africa's locomotives
leased to Zimbabwean railways have been withdrawn during a
period of strained relations. Traffic at the Beitbridge border has

been deliberately slowed down for "customs checks." In view of the region's dependence on South African transport, the disruptive potential of "railway diplomacy" is obvious.

All this enhances the resolve of the black community throughout the region to unite and achieve majority rule in South Africa. But it has also had another important consequence: it has caused the two superpowers to become more involved in the region. South African incursions into Angola gave the Cubans the "moral cover" to intrude. South African support for UNITA has also contributed to a continuous Soviet presence in Angola. This, in turn, causes the United States to consider southern Africa in the context of East-West relations, an unwelcome complication in a region that has enough problems already.

The close interconnection among all the countries of southern Africa and the dominance of South Africa over all of them are facts of life. The independence that exists for the states surrounding South Africa is a political independence, but their freedom of action is severely constrained by the vast imbalance between their resources and those of South Africa. This constraint confines their policy options within narrow limits in many critical areas, which is especially galling for them because of their natural hostility to everything the South African government stands for. Their dependence on South Africa in so many respects also means that any policy toward South Africa must be measured in its effects upon and implications for their own countries.

The Strategic Significance of Southern Africa

South Africa is the source of a number of minerals essential to Western industry, including the defense industry. Such supplies could be cut off by a decision of the South African government or by a breakdown of law and order that would prevent the mining of these minerals or their transport or export. These are therefore important matters for the Western alliance. It is unlikely, however, that the firms that use the minerals would be living from hand to mouth; they are acutely conscious of the dangers and have been working to maintain reserves. The longer the interruption of supplies, the more serious the consequences, since reserves would be steadily exhausted. Yet neither the present white South African government nor any future black successor would have any interest in denying itself the substantial foreign exchange earnings of mineral export industries. The most serious risk is perhaps that of a prolonged breakdown of internal order, in which the interruption of mineral supplies would only be one among several Western concerns.

The Cape Sea route is of acknowledged strategic importance for the West, and the huge expansion of the Soviet Navy can only be interpreted as a threat to such key Western strategic areas. The Cape, however, is not likely to be a high Soviet priority because it would be hard to stop the passage of all shipping in the vast areas of sea south of the Cape and, even if successful, the blockade would be of little significance except in a long-term conventional war, the least likely eventuality. There are other better places that the Soviet Navy could use as choke points for Western shipping.

The loss to the communist world of southern Africa as a whole would be a major blow and is something that the South African government clearly fears. In Angola in 1975 the Soviet Union demonstrated its readiness to act with great promptness through its surrogates, the Cubans, in support of an opportunity they saw open to them. The fear is, so the argument goes, that given the chance Moscow would do the same again in South Africa. But the Soviets' commitment of resources would have to be substantially greater in any intervention on the scale required to tilt the balance in an area as large as South Africa.

On the contrary, there is mounting evidence that Mr. Gorbachev's priorities are internal and economic; he would thus like to reduce the Soviet Union's external commitments, especially those that are expensive, profitless, and liable to put at risk other more important interests. For South Africa, the surprising message is that the Soviet Union would not want to see a general collapse or bloodbath over the apartheid issue. Gorbachev has specifically said that the Soviet Union must not do anything to bring it about. He favors a peaceful solution, though he is not hopeful about the prospects.

Such matters are decided in the Soviet Union on a cool calculation of advantage, and the present situation is not without its attractions. The Soviet Union does not need to do anything, and yet can snipe at the West. However, Gorbachev must have reasoned that in the event of a breakdown he would not want to find himself in a position where he either had to reveal his weakness by declining appeals for help or risk a superpower confrontation by intervening, when he could hardly rate highly his chances of success if he did.

Other considerations that may have carried weight are the Soviet interest not to upset the current arrangements for marketing gold, diamonds, and some other precious minerals, and the wider implications for the world economy of violence and uncertainty in South Africa. The Soviet Union will certainly want to be in good standing with the government of a post-apartheid South Africa, but it may have decided, rightly, that such an interest, too, would be best served by a birth without avoidable pain.

One of the lessons of history is that the West should never lower its guard in dealing with the communist world. How long this new Soviet policy will last remains to be seen. But there is enough evidence of change to see what the implications may be for the ANC, which is pledged to armed struggle (with Soviet support and arms!), and whether South Africa will revise the concept of total onslaught. The South African government presents itself as the only bastion against the extension of Soviet influence in the region, and it played on this theme during the elections in May 1987 with a good deal of scaremongering. The ANC under its present leadership remains essentially African Nationalist; the influence of the Communist Party is significant rather than dominant. It must be remembered that the majority of South African blacks are profoundly religious and have Western values. In South Africa 75 percent of the blacks and 90 percent of the whites are churchgoers. The danger for the South African government is that, ironically, by refusing to negotiate with the Nationalist leadership it may be turning its own allegations into a self-fulfilling prophecy.

The scope for Soviet influence in the region is circumscribed by economic and political circumstances. The best Soviet opportunities have arisen through the withdrawal of Portugal from Angola, where the Soviet position is underpinned by the presence of Cuban troops, and from Mozambique, where the introduction of a Marxist regime in 1975 was a coup. However, the Soviet Union has been unable to provide the economic support that developing nations require, and it cannot in practice compete with the West as a diplomatic power in the region. It must remain a major objective of Western policy to ensure that disagreements between the West and the Front Line States do not allow the Soviet Union to build effective regional influence by default.

The Imperative of Acting Together

Against this background, the first issue is the precise objectives that we seek to achieve. First and foremost is the dismantling of apartheid. Second, and equally important, is to try to achieve the dismantling of apartheid by peaceful means and to set an example for others. We should not resign ourselves to the inevitability of violence. The interests of everyone are best served by maintaining the greatest degree of political stability that is possible. The issue of sanctions must be considered in this context. Third, the interconnection of all countries in the subcontinent must not be forgotten. The consequences for surrounding countries of any action taken in relation to South Africa must always be weighed. This means that any policy toward South Africa must fit into a coherent strategy for the whole region. Fourth, it is crucial that the Western nations act together—no easy task given the differences of perception, interest, and history that exist among them in relation to South Africa. Yet the more concerted the action of whatever nature, the greater the impact. The confused collection of policies in place at present is not effective and enables the South African government to play off one country against another.

The most public aspect of difference within the alliance is the issue of sanctions. But the allies differ on other aspects, too: in approaches to aid, to the Front Line States, and to trade and investment issues. They also differ in their appreciation of "liberation" movements. The result is virtually no impact on South Africa. Even working in cooperation the extent of possible leverage is small, and it must be a policy objective to maximize it. Otherwise, what is the meaning of the calls to end apartheid?

It is expecting too much to think that all countries can take identical action, but the time has come for coordinated action within a defined strategy common to all. Political will can overcome the difficulties of such coordination. A coherent, complementary, and sustainable Western approach to South Africa would dispel any lingering doubt in that country that in the fight against apartheid we are all on the side of those South Africans—black and white—who are working for fundamental change. The message to South Africa would be more forceful than anything sent so far.

Will the quest for a concerted strategy produce strains within the alliance? Here it is essential to think clearly about definitions. South Africa is not a subject for NATO, which has a specific role laid down by treaty to provide its sixteen member nations with an integrated defense capability that will deter any perceived threat of aggression. It would be extraordinarily unwise to divert NATO's energies toward South Africa—a problem that does not represent a threat and does not call for action in the context of the North Atlantic Treaty. South Africa is the "out of area" problem par excellence: it is unrelated to NATO's role except in the most marginal way. It would be folly to impose on NATO any extraneous strain of this kind.

However, this does not mean that the South Africa issue is not of vital importance to every member of the Western alliance and to all democracies everywhere. The rights of individuals and freedom of speech are the core of our democratic values for which millions have died. In that sense, present conditions in South Africa disturb the conscience of every free nation. If the Western democracies are genuine in their desire to change those conditions, then the logic leads to more positive and concerted political action. In Western Europe the vehicle for concerted action is the European Community and its political cooperation. NATO as such does not come into it. The strains will arise in the context of a wider international effort to bring change to South Africa. Such strains are not desirable but cannot be shirked.

Poor Choices: Sanctions, White Reform, Black Power

In the light of all these circumstances, the realistic choices are few. An example underscores the difficulty. Suppose sanctions result in pressure to ban the export to South Africa of some industrial products manufactured in Britain. Suppose also that implementing this ban would cause the collapse of a certain British firm and the loss of a thousand jobs. Let us suppose also that no reasonable case can be made for saying that the ban of the export of the products in question would have the slightest effect on persuading the South African government to abandon apartheid—in other words, that the ban would be a pointless but costly gesture. Suppose that I am the Member of Parliament for the constituency where that firm is located: should I feel guilty in opposing that ban?

The case for comprehensive mandatory economic sanctions—imposed by the Security Council on all UN members under Chapter VII of the UN Charter, rather than the voluntary measures that some countries or groups of countries have decided to impose on their own initiative—is that collective pressure is needed to force the South Africans to accept fundamental change; and that, if violence is ruled out, economic sanctions are the only other form of pressure. Certainly there is scope for applying economic pressure, but the question is one of scale. It would be convenient if the South African problem could be dealt with peacefully by universally applied stringent sanctions. The screws would be turned, no one would get hurt—at least not so as anyone would notice—and all would miraculously change.

Would that it were so. But is it? Historical experience has shown that mandatory sanctions seldom achieve the desired effect. They are most likely to do so if the target country is small and vulnerable, if the sanctions can have immediate and penetrating effect, and if the objective is limited. None of these conditions apply in the case of South Africa. It is a large and powerful country with a high degree of self-sufficiency, which laid its plans long ago to withstand sanctions. The bulk of its exports are in gold and strategic minerals, commodities well suited to sanction busting. To the extent that sanctions have some economic effect, the jobs and welfare of the black population and the surrounding countries would also be affected. That is a price that might have to be paid, but unfortunately there are other aspects and consequences of sanctions that must be measured.

The white population would naturally consider its vital interests at stake. The shape of its future is bound to matter more than limited economic hardship. South Africa is not just another colonial problem. Most of its white population has no other country to go to and no desire to leave South Africa. It is therefore simply unrealistic to think that the South African government would respond to foreign boycotts and sanctions by making the reforms we want. More likely, such pressures would have the opposite result, pushing whites to develop a siege economy. The swing to the right in the 1987 white elections indicates a diminishing rather than an increasing international influence over the actions of South Africa.

Then there is enforcement. In practice, large numbers of countries, including many of those most vocal in demanding sanctions, will continue to trade with South Africa in one way or another. In many cases their economic circumstances leave them no alternative—a fact shown all too clearly in the case of Rhodesia (Zimbabwe). Middlemen quickly emerged to find ways around sanctions. The same would happen with South Africa, and perhaps even more so.

Despite evasion, sanctions still might have a significant economic impact. The South African authorities would transfer the additional costs on to the black population and neighboring countries so far as they could, rather than allow the burden to fall on their own people. The lack of growth would result in increased unemployment, fewer resources for black education, housing and other services, and—perhaps worst of all—large scale repatriation of black workers to neighboring states and to the homelands.

A high rate of economic growth is needed just to keep up with the annual growth in the black work force; without it the social and economic consequences for the blacks would be severe. Economic growth has been a direct stimulus to the forces for change in South Africa. It has led to increasing black economic power, the emergence of black trade unions, and improved facilities for black education and training. It is argued that all this only strengthens apartheid, but the evidence suggests that industrialization has served to weaken racial barriers and to promote reform as the needs of a modern industrial society override political dogma. The dynamic of events place an increasing strain on apartheid itself, which is precisely the development we wish to encourage.

So far as surrounding countries are concerned, South Africans have already given notice to the world that if sanctions were applied they would "not be in a position to continue giving loans and financial aid to neighboring states."[1] They would give preference to their own work force at the expense of hundreds of thousands of expatriate workers. They have warned of the possibility of cutting trade with neighboring states and severing transport links. If this happened, the only other rail links would be the already stretched lines to Beira and Dar-es-Salaam, and the disrupted Benguela, Limpopo, and Nacala lines. If South Africa takes all these actions or even only a few of them, the potential damage to the economies of the Front Line States would be considerable. The social consequences would be incalculable.

If the white rulers of South Africa will not be moved by economic sanctions, and if in a general sense the threat of sanctions makes them even less willing to do what we want, does it follow that Western countries should encourage the Afrikaners' own internal moves toward reform? It can be argued that the South African government is proceeding as far and as fast as it knows to be possible, and that for want of anything better we should encourage it and be patient.

Such support might range, at one extreme, from open and positive support for the South African government, perhaps combined with a recognition that it is a pro-Western regime opposed to communism, and at the other extreme, to a mild version of constructive engagement. However, the South African government has so far given us no reason to think that it will go as far as we know to be necessary, even if some progress has been made. Moreover, the West cannot appear to be supporting the policies of a regime it rejects as unacceptable. We must continue trying to persuade them to change their ways, without making the mistake of thinking that the South African government will reward us in any material sense for supporting them.

A Policy for the Western Alliance

Yet neither can any member of the Western alliance support the violent overthrow of the South African government that many black South Africans and blacks in Africa advocate. The West cannot support a policy that would be contrary to the UN Charter. It is a beguiling but false argument to think that a short, sharp, violent conflict will topple the regime with less damage and loss of life than a prolonged escalating conflict. It may be difficult, and may well become considerably more difficult, for the West to come out in sympathy with the blacks while distancing itself from violence. Frustration may impel the blacks to pursue an increasingly extreme policy with which the West will feel progressively more uncomfortable. But violence and extremism must be rejected.

What *is* a valid choice for the Western alliance is to demonstrate sympathy and practical support for the South African blacks who are recognized as valid representatives, and use all its influence to promote negotiations to replace apartheid by a genuinely democratic nonracial system of government. The West could be quite open with this demonstration, which would go some way to correct the clear impression held by the blacks that its anti-apartheid position is hypocritical: strong on words and weak on action.

This policy, which would be in part an attitudinal change, would make the West better placed to influence the blacks the sooner it comes out in their support. Furthermore, the moderate blacks are more likely to prevail if the West has espoused the black cause in general, which does not mean supporting blacks in every particular; on the contrary, we must feel able to criticize, even to condemn, what we see as undesirable in black policies, pronouncements or actions.

Such a policy would fit with the requirements imposed by two important premises: the need for the outside world to bear upon South Africa in the most effective way to bring about peaceful change as soon as possible; and the acceptance of the fact that results cannot be quick. The first requirement is the need for concerted action. The second is political: bringing the public's hopes into harmony with what it will be possible to achieve in practice. Our collective power to bring about change is limited. The situation is in no way comparable to, say, the Philippines or South Korea where fundamental change followed weeks or months of popular demonstrations witnessed on television by the whole world. The army and police in South Africa are closely white-controlled and will remain so.

The process of dismantling apartheid has been and will continue to be gradual, and this policy choice would fit exactly with that. The policy would give a positive push to a process that will lead eventually to the desired result. As each step is taken so the next can be considered in the context of the circumstances at the time. And circumstances will change, not only in southern Africa but elsewhere as well. Western leadership itself will change and the attitudes of electorates will also evolve. The Soviet Union is attempting change but it is only possible to second guess the result. The U.S. presidential election will cause an uneasy stability in 1988, but beyond that lies uncertainty. A world recession is clearly a possibility and the extent to which it can be alleviated or even prevented remains to be seen.

The Western approach should be directed by four guiding principles. First, there is no reason that overt support for the blacks should mean any less willingness on the part of the West to engage in peaceful dialogue; quite the contrary. Peaceful dialogue means patient advocacy with all sides, whether the South African government, the blacks or whites in South Africa, the other races, the ANC or any other organization. Nothing will be gained by excluding any major party from such dialogue because in the end only a change that commands the broad support of *all* South Africans can be expected to endure.

One of the strengths of the West is that it has a large number of contacts outside government that can be brought to bear. In four areas in particular an active policy of dialogue could be most usefully advanced: first, in the academic world in South Africa where genuine new thinking is taking place; second, in the trade unions that are at an early formative stage in South Africa and that could well benefit from increased Western contact; third, in the business community where Western industrial and commercial leaders could have a thoroughly healthy influence on their South African counterparts; and fourth, perhaps most importantly, in the churches where there is a large group of people who should be in favor of justice, goodwill, cooperation, and peace. Admittedly there are enormous divisions among different denominations of the church, but a conscious effort, especially with the backing of the churches outside South Africa, to heal the divisions of the churches inside South Africa might open far-reaching possibilities.

The second guiding principle of a concerted policy is a coordinated international aid program for the entire southern African region. Some countries already provide aid on a substantial scale, but the total is not commensurate with needs in the context of ending apartheid. Whatever economic pressure is applied to South Africa, the effects will be felt in all the surrounding countries. It would be neither right nor possible to protect those countries from the consequences of any action they themselves took toward South Africa, but to the extent that they would be affected by the actions of the West toward South Africa, their need for aid would increase. As those countries are so enthusiastic for action against South Africa, they would no doubt accept some extra hardship. But for the West's policy to be coherent and effective, it must take into account all the circumstances throughout the region. A policy that exerted pressure on South Africa but neglected the damaging consequences of that on other countries would not be coherent.

So, more needs to be done. This applies particularly to the United States where Congress imposed sanctions but failed to increase aid. The British program of bilateral and multilateral aid to the member states of the Southern African Development Coordination Conference was almost two billion dollars over the seven-year period 1980–1987. Pledges of further support were given in February 1987, most of which have been allocated to improve regional transport and communications. The policy objective here is to lessen the dependence of neighboring countries on South Africa. If the United States and other countries weighed in with proportionate contributions, much more progress would be possible.

Another aspect of the need to make the Front Line States less dependent on South Africa is military. Here again, the British are playing a constructive role; British training teams have been in Zimbabwe since 1980. There is no comparable U.S. assistance and no apparent understanding of the need. Military security is no less vital to those countries than it is to the member states of NATO. Security is also important in the matter of investment. Ideally, the companies that have disinvested in South Africa should reinvest in one of the neighboring countries. But they have not done so, nor has foreign private capital been forthcoming for other ventures. Lack of security is part of the reason.

The other important aspect of aid is education and training for blacks in South Africa. Much is done here already but obviously more could be done with long-term advantage.

Third, even though mandatory economic sanctions are unwise, there is an important place for economic pressure that does not have the damaging consequences of full-scale sanctions. A number of countries have taken restrictive measures toward South Africa, including discouraging sports events, cultural and scientific contacts, and banning military cooperation, oil exports and new nuclear collaboration. Britain has, in addition, imposed a ban on new government loans to the South African government and its agencies and ceased providing funding for trade missions.

The U.S. Congress has imposed more severe restrictions; for example, bans on the import of South African agricultural products, uranium, coal, and textiles; on U.S. bank loans to South Africa and U.S. government procurement from South Africa; and on air links and the promotion of tourism. The European Community has not gone as far, but it has banned exports of sensitive equipment and the import of gold coins, iron, and steel and also new investment. The Dutch, the French, and the Irish have done more on their own initiative, while the major Nordics in general support all the measures that have been discussed internationally, notably a total trade ban.

Those who wish to see far more extensive sanctions in place cannot be content with this list. They are not prepared even to acknowledge that much more drastic action could have tragic or even catastrophic results. However, it would be wrong to assume either that existing restrictions do not have some effect in South Africa or that the limits of economic action it is safe to take have been reached. The beginnings of a changing attitude by some of the more liberally minded whites and others within South Africa are unmistakable. The evidence is mainly anecdotal but no less poignant. The meetings between South African businessmen and the ANC in Zambia in 1985 and more recently in Senegal are only one indication of change. The South African government seeks to dismiss such events, but they cannot be dismissed. These traces of a changing outlook cannot be claimed as a direct result of economic action by the outside world, but there is no reason to doubt that it contributes to change.

In addition to action by governments, there is disinvestment by the private sector. Such decisions are taken in the end on the basis of hard commercial judgment, but the inspiration for them flows from the deep dislike of the South African regime felt by hundreds of thousands of people who have dealings with companies. The private sector has felt itself driven to respond to the general public pressure to "do" something. For this reason disinvestment is likely to continue. It results in the absorption of indigenous resources that would otherwise be channeled into new investment—creating new jobs. Disinvestment also results in the substitution of white South African ownership for a foreign ownership that is being increasingly compelled by its own public to do all it can to help the blacks. Neither of these results is desirable. The economic and social consequences of disinvestment are difficult to measure, and it is impossible to identify in advance at what stage in the process the damage will become excessive and counterproductive. That stage does not yet appear to have been reached, but it is a danger that must be watched with great care.

The fourth guiding principle is to prepare beforehand for each successive stage as apartheid diminishes. Each stage does not leave a void: something else must replace it and that must be thought about in advance. Beyond that, the nonracial democratic system of government that will come after apartheid should be thought about now. We know how difficult that will prove because of the unique mixture of races in South Africa—all the more reason to work on such a system now. The problem has not received enough attention yet, especially from the black community. The more the black community can demonstrate to the rest of the world the kind of fair-minded democracy it seeks, the more likely is support for the cause to be forthcoming. Other governments with experience in these matters can help, if the South Africans—black or white—want help, but they must not prescribe specific constitutional structures. That is for all South Africans themselves to decide.

Some attention has recently been given to the drafting of statements of principles. Several of these suggest that the white community, if it agreed to the dismantling of apartheid, would nevertheless retain a protected position. It is important to be careful about any such notion because no one in the West has any authority or standing to negotiate on behalf of anyone in South Africa. We must all be scrupulous in going no further than to call for the establishment of a nonracial democratic system of government. At the same time there is an urgent need to put some clothing on that outline. This would have a very powerful influence on how the struggle to end apartheid by peaceful means is carried on. The void that exists today needs to be filled, and the blacks must understand that.

There is a final point to be made here. We should not forget the value of inducements, the carrot as well as the stick. The most powerful inducement we can offer to all South Africans is the prospect of an end to the agony of apartheid, and to the whites in particular the prospect of a welcome back into the fraternity of the free world with all the benefits that that could bring them—if only they would abandon apartheid. It would cost us nothing to say this. Indeed, within that broad inducement there is a strong case for linking some specific steps with specific inducements. For example, as an inducement to abolish the Group Areas Act, the European Community could undertake to help in material ways with the enormous problems in housing and health that will ensue; or in response to the desegregation of education, there could be commitment to a program of technical aid to bring the blacks up to the same level as the whites. There are a number of such possibilities that should be considered and that fit precisely into the strategy of setting in motion a process that would lead to the end of apartheid.

The strategy suggested here is rooted in the reality on the ground in southern Africa. It thus has formidable implications for national leaders and politicians, who have the responsibility of bridging the gap between what so many of their electorates want to happen and what it is possible to achieve. The natural, emotive concern felt by so many people over the suffering and injustice in South Africa, which drives them to clamor for more and more action, must be tempered by the truth that unless great care is taken, the situation could be made worse, perhaps even far worse, leading to bloodshed. No responsible government should advocate such a course.

The challenge this represents to politicians in relation to their public opinions is immense. This is true for every country, but especially for the United States because of the facts of its domestic political life. The rest of the world must understand this. In the United States such a task is likely to be possible only if the international policy toward South Africa is as positive and strong as is practical.

The strategy advocated here has a theme: pressure, perseverance, and patience. All three should be emphasized, but above all patience. The dynamic of human affairs is working in the right direction in South Africa. Change will come. We want to hasten it if we can, but peacefully. All races, all groups, all sections of South African society are South Africans. All have their distinctive contribution to make to their country, one of extraordinary grandeur and richness. Their future lies in living and working together as a nation in harmony with itself. However unlikely it may seem, the hope that the South African government and its electors may yet be brought to see the inevitability and the wisdom of peaceful change must not be discarded. Somehow among us all and with the help of South Africans themselves, we must find the best ways to support and succor the whole region through the deepest and longest crisis of its turbulent history.

Note

1. UN Security Council, August 29, 1985.

Breaking the Laager:
A Two-track Western Policy
toward South Africa

Max van der Stoel

Much as opinions in the West differ on how to tackle the problem of South Africa, there is virtual unanimity that the present situation is untenable. Few people doubt that a long and bloody struggle is likely to become inevitable if no speedy solution is reached by way of negotiations. Even Secretary of State George Shultz, usually so cautious in his choice of words, expressed himself in unequivocal terms on this point when he said in December 1986 that "delay only invites disaster."[1]

But is it likely that a speedy solution can be reached? On the basis of an analysis of recent events in South Africa, I can only come to a pessimistic conclusion. The South African government has paid more attention to repression than to reform. And the few reforms that were implemented were of secondary importance. The government clearly wants to maintain the privileged position of the white minority. It seems more interested in splitting the black majority than in opening a genuine dialogue.

The Primacy of White Rights

Over the last few years, violence has increased in South Africa. Thousands of black South Africans have fallen victim to the actions of police and army. The ANC, banned by the government but undoubtedly assured of the sympathy of a very large section of the black population, has ceased to limit its activities to civil disobedience, as in past years, and in the absence of substantial reforms has begun to resort to violence. If whites and blacks cannot manage to reduce the tensions in South African society by means of a process of negotiation soon, this violence threatens to escalate into civil war.

49

The present situation is especially intolerable because the whites, only about one-seventh of the total population, wish to preserve their privileged positions of authority in state and society. While white supremacy in the rest of Africa has disappeared during the last few decades, the blacks in South Africa, making up almost three-fourths of the total population, are deprived of the right to participate in elections to the South African Parliament; and despite all President Botha's assurances about his devotion to democratic values, over 86 percent of the territory of South Africa, including all areas possessing major natural resources or industrial development, have been declared "white." The remaining 13 percent, the poorest areas in South Africa, have been divided into ten so-called black homelands. Four of these have been proclaimed independent states—even though a cursory glance at the map shows that these islands in the middle of the area declared "white" cannot possibly attain any true exercise of sovereignty. As a consequence of pseudo-independence, the inhabitants of these homelands have lost their South African citizenship and become aliens in their own land.

In order to make the separation of the races as complete as possible, the so-called Group Areas Act was introduced. Under this Act, between 1960 and 1983, 3.5 million black people were transferred to a different residential area, often by force. Since 1983 this number has risen still further. In this way, hundreds of thousands of black people have been compelled to travel for many hours each day to and from their new place of residence, or else to spend their leisure time separated from their families in miserable dormitories.

The differences in the standard of living between black and white workers are also great. The average white employee earns four times as much as the average black worker. The social emancipation of the black population is impeded by the generally inferior quality of the education they receive. The state spends on average four and a half times as much on the education of each white as on each black child. Even those black people who have succeeded in obtaining a proper education often face a bleak future in the job market.

In a 1986 speech that gave more satisfaction to President Botha than to black leaders within or outside South Africa, President Reagan declared, "The realization has come hard and late, but the realization has finally come to Pretoria that apartheid belongs to the past."[2] He then proceeded to list the changes that had occurred over the last few years in Pretoria. He pointed to the development of a black trade union movement; to the abolition of the laws prohibiting marriage and sexual relations between the races; and to the disappearance of the infamous pass laws, infringements of which led to the arrest of 1.9 million black people in the years between 1975 and 1984. These are indeed developments that should not be ignored. But apart from a softening of some of its aspects, the government does not show any inclination to end the system of apartheid.

When President Botha wrote in December 1985 to the Commonwealth Group of Eminent Persons that the South African government was "reconciled to the eventual disappearance of white domination," there seemed compelling reasons for the government to move in that direction: growing resistance from and steadily increasing bitterness among the black population; the fact that in the year 2000, according to demographic projections, whites would make up only 10 percent of the total population of the country; and the isolation into which the apartheid policy had led South Africa internationally. Nevertheless, the Commonwealth Group was forced in its final report to come to the conclusion that the South African government was "not yet prepared to negotiate fundamental change, nor to countenance the creation of genuine democratic structures, nor to face the prospect of the end of white domination and white power in the foreseeable future. Its program of reform does not end apartheid, but seeks to give it a less inhuman face. Its quest is power-sharing, but without surrendering overall white control."

It is difficult for anyone who examines the attitude of the South African government to reach any other conclusion. The "one man, one vote" principle is simply rejected out of hand. The government clings to the 1984 constitution and its three racially-defined chambers, with their decision-making procedures and powers so defined that in case of any conflict of opinion the white chamber almost always has the final say. The government refuses to abandon the concept of the homelands— a desperate attempt to reduce the preponderance of the black majority. The millions of blacks outside the homelands are offered no more than some degree of local autonomy in the internal administration of black townships, and the consultation on reforms in an advisory National Statutory Council with "decent, balanced and peace-loving blacks," as President Botha put it in an election speech in May 1987.[3] Even the moderate Chief Buthelezi, head of the government of the KwaZulu homeland, considered the government proposals completely inadequate and described them as an attempt "to divide and rule."

The meagerness of the government's desire for reform was shown once again when representatives of various population groups and Chief Buthelezi's Inkatha reached agreement in November 1986 on a proposal to unite Natal and the KwaZulu homeland. A provincial legislature was to be created with two chambers, one of which would be elected on the basis of the "one man, one vote" principle (and thus possess a black majority), while in the other, also directly elected, the various racial and ethnic groups would have an equal number of seats. In addition, each group would possess the right of veto on matters affecting its religion, language, and cultural and other rights.[4] This formula, Inkatha's idea of a multiracial South African state with a federal structure, met with opposition from the ANC and the UDF, who are in favor of the concept of a unitary state and are afraid that any step toward a federal system would aid the South African government in sowing divisions in the black population. But it soon became evident that the government considered the plan too radical. What finally emerged on November 3, 1987, was only a Joint Executive Authority that has no legislative powers at all but that will administer "joint affairs" of Natal and KwaZulu, such as the public health service, road construction, and maintenance.

The pattern of South African government policy becomes ever clearer. On the one hand, the constitutional mechanism introduced in 1984 ensures that so-called "general affairs" remain firmly in white hands; on the other, in treating "group affairs," all white interests considered essential are safeguarded. The Group Areas Act is kept intact, aside from minor concessions. During his party's congress in October 1986, President Botha himself emphasized that this law would remain in force for the rest of his lifetime.[5] The continuing forced removals of tens of thousands of black people throws a shadow over concessions like the Restoration of South African Citizenship Bill of 1986, which gives blacks working and living with their families in the cities the chance to regain their South African citizenship lost when the homelands were declared independent. The significance of this step, which affects 1,750,000 black people, must in any case be seen against the fact that for more than 7 million blacks the loss of South African citizenship is not being reversed.

Where the government has made concessions, they seem to be prompted primarily by the recognition that blacks are indispensable as workers in South African economy, and that it is impossible to concentrate the entire black population in the homelands. But these reforms are too limited and come too late to satisfy the great majority of blacks. They do lead, however, to acute tensions between the small black minority prepared to place itself at the service of the government and the rest of the black population.

Since the failure of the Commonwealth mission to South Africa in 1986, the situation in the country has deteriorated further, events clearly detailed in other chapters of this book. Several events underscore the government's unwillingness to contemplate real movement.

In November 1987, President Botha released Govan Mbeki, a 77-year-old former Chairman of the ANC, who had been imprisoned with Nelson Mandela since 1964. He did so without insisting, as he had done before, that Mr. Mbeki unconditionally reject violence as a political instrument. This prompted immediate speculation that President Botha, perhaps encouraged by the decline of political unrest in the black townships during 1987, was cautiously preparing the way for the release of Nelson

Mandela and ultimately for a political dialogue with the ANC leaders. However, this optimism was dashed by measures that prevented Mbeki from playing any public role. If Mr. Mandela, who is approaching 70, were released, a similar fate would await him. A exploration of ways to open a dialogue with the ANC is clearly not on the government's agenda.

From time to time, there has been speculation that Botha might seek a deal with Chief Buthelezi, considered by Pretoria to be the leader of the six million Zulus, and that Buthelezi might be offered a seat in the cabinet. This prospect is viewed with alarm by the ANC and the UDF, who fear that such a "white-Zulu" alliance would fragment the black majority; tensions between the UDF and Inkhatha have already led to an underground war claiming hundreds of lives.

However, Botha and Buthelezi still seem far apart. Botha made it clear that he still is not prepared to make substantial concessions to Buthelezi when he shelved the plan for a joint legislative Council of Natal and KwaZulu. For his part, Buthelezi, confronted with signs of dwindling support in towns like Durban and Pietermaritzburg, cannot afford to be too forthcoming. In December 1987, having earlier indicated that he would not be willing to take a seat in the proposed National Advisory Council until Nelson Mandela and other black political leaders were released, Buthelezi said bluntly that it would be "suicidal" for him to enter negotiations as long as the government refused to deal with the reality of a black majority.[6]

Warning Signs for Botha

For the immediate future the position of the South African government seems to be invulnerable. In the coming years, the National Party can count on an ample majority in the white chamber of parliament—certainly if, as seems likely, it succeeds in deferring new elections to this body until 1992. Repression of black resistance has weakened its organizational structure. At the same time, longer-term developments must give the government cause for considerable concern.

In the first place, dialogue with the black community presents a dilemma. If the government persists in its present attitude, the chances of restoring stability in the country seem to be near zero. This inability to achieve a settlement with the blacks and their leaders cannot fail to have a negative effect on the South African economy. As fears grow that the polarization between black and white will lead to a disaster for South Africa, there can be no hope of substantial investments from abroad, even if foreign governments did not try to stop them. Average growth of GNP was only 1 percent in the period 1981–1987, while the average annual growth of the population is about 2.5 percent. Purchasing power dropped by about 17 percent between the beginning of 1981 and the end of 1987. According to official figures, there are 1 1/2 million unemployed in South Africa, but private estimates put the actual number more than two times higher.[7]

Moreover, the black trade union movement, COSATU, grew rapidly in size and influence, so much so that its political activities were banned along with 16 other anti-apartheid groups in 1988. The 21-day mine worker strike in August 1987— organized without strike funds and involving at its peak 340,000 workers—failed to achieve its aim of forcing the employers to agree to bigger wage increases than they had been willing to offer. But neither was COSATU broken. The employers and their organization, the Chamber of Mines, were impressed by the competence of the strike leaders and the hold they had on the miners. Banned or not, the black trade union movement is now a factor to be reckoned with in South Africa.

Notwithstanding the shift to the right in the 1987 elections, the government also faces a countercurrent that, though numerically weak, reflects a growing realization in the academic world and also increasingly in church circles and in the business community that a fundamental change of course is unavoidable. When the situation worsens, these opinions might carry greater weight.

The government must also feel uncomfortable about the fact that the minister of defense had to inform parliament that in January 1985 around 7,500 conscripts—over a quarter of the annual call-up—had failed to report for duty.[8] These figures are no longer made public, but there is evidence that the reluctance to serve in the armed services continues. A survey conducted at the end of 1987 among students at the Rhodes University in Grahamstown showed that more than half of them wanted to emigrate, most of them in order to escape military service.[9]

Uneasiness among the white population about the present situation in South Africa is reflected in recent migration figures. While immigration dropped sharply from 17,284 in 1985 to 6,994 in 1986, emigration rose from 11,401 in 1985 to 13,711 in 1986. The number of professional and technical emigrants in 1986 was twice that in 1985. U.S. Secretary of State George Shultz noted in a 1986 speech that "many of South Africa's most experienced and talented are emigrating,"[10] and another analysis concluded that "more than 300,000 urban whites are considering leaving."[11] Clearly, many South African whites are beginning to lose faith in the future of their country.

Black Resistance—the ANC

When in the spring of 1986 the Commonwealth Group of Eminent Persons visited South Africa, one of its primary aims was to find a way to open up a dialogue between the South African government and the African National Congress (ANC). Underlying this move was the belief that, despite the existence of other movements, the banned ANC apparently enjoys the most support in the black community in South Africa.

By contrast, the United States has strong reservations about the ANC because communists are said to play an important role in it and because its military wing regularly resorts to violence within South Africa. These reservations were expressed in a speech by President Reagan in July 1986: ". . . the South African government is under no obligation to negotiate the future of the country with any organization that proclaims a goal of creating a communist state and uses terrorist tacts and violence to achieve it."[12]

It is undoubtedly true that communists do play a role in the ANC, and it is equally undeniable that the supply of arms to the ANC comes largely from the communist world. Does this mean that the ANC is a willing instrument in the hands of Moscow, as South African government propaganda would have us believe? Foreign Minister Hans-Dietrich Genscher of the Federal Republic noted that many African liberation movements have established links with Moscow, without themselves being communist.[13] Against the South African government claim that no fewer than 23 of the 30 members of the National Executive of the ANC are either members or active supporters of the South African Communist party must be set the recent verdict of an expert on the subject who, after careful research, came to the conclusion that this number was much smaller, probably amounting to no more than 3.[14] The report of the 1986 Commonwealth report quotes a respected South Africa expert on the ANC, Tom Lodge, that this organization is essentially "a movement of pragmatists, not ideologues."

Should the ANC eventually succeed in placing its stamp on some future South African government, it will do so in tandem with the powerful black trade union movement. At present within COSATU there is undoubtedly a good deal of sympathy for radical socioeconomic reforms of a socialist nature, but future union leaders are not likely to support a typical communist state structure with little room for trade unions.

It is, however, possible that future leaders of the black resistance may be more extreme. One of the most striking phenomena in South Africa over the last few years has been the radicalization of young black people. This rising generation may reject the present ANC leadership as too moderate and it might set up a new organization; or the ANC itself may become more radical in order to retain control of the younger generation. Strong communist influences may then emerge. However, the Western world will not avert this danger by maintaining a fearful distance from the ANC, while doing no more than the usual verbal condemnations of apartheid. There will only be an effective counterweight to black radicalization if the actions of the Western democracies convince the black population that the West is no mere passive spectator but rather is seeking to make a genuine contribution to the disappearance of the apartheid regime.

This policy approach should aim to regain black people's confidence in the Western democracies by means of a coordinated Western program of action to press the Pretoria government for concessions. But it should equally try to persuade the black leaders that breaking down white resistance to radical reforms in South Africa also depends on persuading whites that there will be a future for them as equal citizens in South Africa once the white minority regime has disappeared, and that even if they have to renounce their privileged positions of authority, they will be able to preserve their cultural identity. In mid-July 1987, when a number of white South Africans and ANC leaders met in Dakar, one black spokesman commented after the meeting that "it was ironic" that "the victims have to give guarantees before the system of oppression can be displaced."[15]

This attitude is understandable, but still the ANC leadership will have to be persuaded that it is in the interest of the struggle against apartheid that the white population be offered certain guarantees. A large majority of the whites is at present convinced that a disappearance of the current apartheid regime would mean their own ruin—an attitude strengthened by government propaganda that incessantly harps on the claim that a surrender to black demands would result in a communist dictatorship in which the whites would be deprived of all rights. Future meetings between whites and blacks like that in Dakar can play a role in shaking that white conviction. Most observers of South Africa are struck by how little contact there is between blacks and whites and by how little whites know about the living conditions and aspirations of black people. Private organizations, and also churches, can organize these contacts even though the Botha government will undoubtedly do all in its power to impede them.

Can it be said that the ANC is engaged in "terrorism," as the American Comprehensive Anti-Apartheid Act of 1986 suggests? The Reagan Administration did not appear to believe that acts of violence by opposition groups were in all circumstances terrorism; the President himself was in the habit of using the term "freedom fighters" to refer to the contras carrying on an armed struggle against the government of Nicaragua. The ANC resorted to violence only after fundamental human rights had been denied to the black population for many years, after peaceful tactics had achieved no change in the situation, and after the repeated use of brute force by the South African government against black people. The regime in Pretoria provoked the reciprocal use of force by the ANC.

That is not to say that all the tactics adopted should receive our sympathetic understanding. Attacks on civilians and on nonmilitary targets are reprehensible; the barbarous practice of "necklacing" blacks who have placed themselves at the service of the regime deserves sharp condemnation. Even if the use of violence is considered purely from the point of view of its effectiveness in the struggle against apartheid, there is good reason for anxiety. It should be remembered that the struggle between the government's well-organized security apparatus and the ANC guerrillas is unequal, one that frequently leads to an escalation of violence against the black population. More-over, armed attacks reinforce the white populations belief in the government's prophecies of the doom that would befall them in case of surrender to black demands.

Mutual violence eliminates in advance any chance of fruitful dialogue between black and white, a prerequisite for any solution to the conflict in South Africa. That is why in 1986 the Commonwealth Group of Eminent Persons concentrated on looking for a formula to bring an end to the violence. The ANC was asked to show willingness to enter negotiations and to suspend violence. The South African government was to accept the removal of the military from the townships, measures providing for freedom of assembly and discussion, and suspension of detention without trial. The government was also to release Nelson Mandela and other political prisoners and detainees, unban the ANC and PAC, and permit normal political activity.

Mandela, who enjoys a respect among the blacks of South Africa unparalleled by any other leader in the black resistance movement, expressed himself in favor of this proposal, subject to consultations with other ANC leaders. The ANC leadership in exile seemed willing to go along despite its doubts about the good faith of the South African government. Although Botha had earlier written to the Commonwealth that "a suspension of violence is a requirement for dialogue," the South Africa government suddenly insisted that a demand for the *"termination of violence"* should be put to the ANC, thus ending any hope of negotiations. Mandela remained in prison, and the escalation of the conflict continued. Had the proposed formula been accepted by Pretoria, on the other hand, a free Mandela would probably have succeeded in inducing the radical youth to restrain themselves in order that the negotiations should be not disrupted by acts of violence. During the negotiations the South African government would then moreover have found itself sitting opposite, as the head of the black delegation, a man of pronounced democratic convictions.

Nelson Mandela is a man of stature, prestige, and democratic orientation—he said during the trial brought against him in 1964: "From my reading of Marxist literature and from conversations with Marxists, I have gained the impression that communists regard the parliamentary system of the West as undemocratic and reactionary. But, on the contrary, I am an admirer of such a system."[16] He is virtually indispensable to any renewed attempt to avert catastrophe in South Africa. The governments of the United States and of the European Community countries have been right to lay special emphasis on the need for his release during their contacts with the government in Pretoria. But Mandela was equally right in his statement in 1985 when he put forward the demand that his fellow-prisoners should also be released because, in his words, ". . . only free men can negotiate. . . . Prisoners cannot enter into contracts."

Objections to Sanctions

Innumerable resolutions of both the UN General Assembly and its Security Council, pressure over many years by successive American administrations, appeals from the Commonwealth countries and from European Community missions: none have brought Pretoria closer to making fundamental changes in its policy. The reforms that have been introduced have been overshadowed by greater repression in the context of the State of Emergency, which has strengthened the hand of the police and army. The hard facts support the conclusions of the co-chairmen of the Commonwealth Group of Eminent Persons,

Malcolm Fraser and Olusegun Obasango: "Any minimal change which has been achieved in South Africa recently has been as a result of substantial pressures, mostly from within South Africa, not as a result of quiet persuasion."[17]

But is it desirable—and if desirable, possible—to exert enough external pressure on the South African government to force it to make drastic alterations in policy? On this question the West is divided.

Of all the arguments against exerting pressure, the weakest concerns possible consequences for the vital Western shipping routes round the Cape of Good Hope. If these sea routes have to be defended against the communist threat, South Africa assistance is certainly not indispensable. Moreover, it seems unlikely that Pretoria would interfere with Western shipping in retaliation against sanctions, and thereby deliberately run the risk of drastic Western countermeasures.

Then there is the argument that the West is dependent for its supplies of a number of major raw materials on imports from South Africa or from areas in southern Africa that themselves depend on the South African railroads and ports for their transport to the countries of the West. This argument does not carry much weight either. If the South African economy were threatened by sanctions, it would certainly not be an attractive option to the government to reduce further the country's export earnings by halting or in any way hindering the export of these materials.

However, even if South Africa did decide to do so (or if Western governments, perhaps under pressure from their parliaments, were to feel obliged to impose a complete trade embargo), the consequences for the Western economies would be less serious than is generally supposed. Take the example of three minerals considered to be of great importance for U.S. national defense: manganese, chromium, and platinum. What would happen if imports of these minerals from South and/or southern Africa were to cease completely, remembering that the United States does not like to depend on imports from communist countries? For manganese, in 1983–1985, 62 percent of demand was met through imports from outside South or southern Africa and the communist world. The corresponding figures for chromium and platinum are much lower, 14 percent and 27 percent respectively.[18] However, the United States possesses large stockpiles of various minerals, including enough chromium for 26 months and platinum for 10 months.[19] Finally, for many minerals it is possible to use or develop substitutes; the United States Mineral Advisory Board estimates, for example, that "over 30% of current consumption of chromium could be replaced immediately by available substitutes and that in five to ten years some two-thirds of total consumption could be replaced by the substitutes currently recognized."[20]

The 1987 report of the Secretary of State's Advisory Committee on South Africa came to the unanimous conclusion about the loss of imports that "the potential impact of such a denial is not sufficient cause to determine U.S. policy towards South Africa."[21] There seems to be no reason to come to different conclusions for Europe or Japan. As a precaution, however, it would be advisable to maintain adequate stocks of such minerals—a policy that only France has consistently followed.[22]

Among the Western countries, Britain is the most concerned about the possible consequences of extensive sanctions for its economy. Unemployment might rise as a result of sanctions on firms with important trade relationships with South Africa. According to the United Kingdom-South Africa Trade Association, at the end of 1985 British investments in South Africa "represented more than 40 percent of all foreign investments in that country and more than 7 percent of all British investments overseas."[23] Since then, however, substantial disinvestment has taken place. At the end of 1986, for instance, Barclays Bank sold off its South African interests; and in August 1987, Standard Chartered Bank followed suit.

Moreover, is it sufficient simply to estimate possible economic damage to the United Kingdom in case of far-reaching sanctions? Should consideration not also be given to the potential damage to British interests if the West fails to prevent catastrophe in South Africa? In this context, one of the conclusions of the report of the Commonwealth Group of Eminent Persons— also signed by Lord Barber, who as former Chancellor of the

Exchequer and Chairman of the Standard Chartered Bank is particularly well informed about British interests in South Africa—deserves particular attention: "We are convinced that the South African government is concerned about the adoption of effective economic measures against it. If it comes to the conclusion that it would always remain protected from such measures, the process of change is unlikely to increase in momentum and the descent into violence would be accelerated. In these circumstances, the cost in lives may have to be counted in millions."

Quite a different sort of argument against sanctions is that they are morally unacceptable in view of their adverse effects on the standard of living of the blacks in South Africa. This has been emphasized by Mrs. Thatcher and backed by President Reagan. "The Prime Minister of Great Britain had denounced punitive sanctions as 'immoral' and 'utterly repugnant'," he said in 1986, "Well, let me tell you why we believe Mrs. Thatcher is right. The primary victims of an economic boycott of South Africa would be the very people we seek to help."[24]

But is it justified to condemn sanctions against South Africa as immoral when most black leaders in South Africa do not share this opinion and even call for sanctions themselves? Are economic sanctions, given their potential consequences for innocent people, always fundamentally wrong? They are not *always* wrong in the eyes of the Reagan Administration, considering the economic measures it has taken against Nicaragua. And how can Mrs. Thatcher's statements about the harm of sanctions be reconciled with other statements she has made, for instance suggesting that sanctions would not work anyway: "South Africa has colossal internal resources. A colossal cost line. And whatever sanctions were put on, materials would get in and out."[25] Last but not least, what alternative is offered by those who reject sanctions? In fact it is little more than a continuation of the policy of public appeals and discrete diplomatic pressures that have so obviously failed to produce any significant results.

Current Sanctions

For many years, the only sanctions applied to South Africa were on the exports of arms, decided upon by the Security Council in its resolution 418 of 1977. Pressures by parliaments and public opinion induced the governments of the member states of the European Community and United States to take some steps, but they were of minor significance. When pressures mounted in 1986 as a consequence of further deterioration in South Africa, significant new measures were decided—but not without considerable differences of view. As a result there is no concerted policy on the part of South Africa's principal trading partners.

Within the European Community, the Netherlands took the lead in insisting on meaningful sanctions. This stand reflected the strong revulsion that the system of apartheid has caused among the Dutch, a revulsion also reflected in almost continuous public discussion and frequent parliamentary debates on the subject. Denmark and Ireland also took a strong position in favor of more sanctions. In September 1986 the EEC finally decided to add to earlier measures—such as bans on the export to South Africa of any crude oil circulating in the free market of the member states and on any further cooperation with South Africa in the nuclear field—a ban on new investments in South Africa and on the import of iron and steel (amounting to about $356 million) from that country. It is, however, doubtful that these steps will have much impact. The ban on the import of steel was weakened because steel alloys were excluded. And given the tensions in South Africa, there was already a sharp decline in West European interest in fresh investments in that country.

Moreover, it also proved impossible for the EEC heads of governments to agree in June 1986 to a ban on the import of coal into the European Community, no doubt much to Pretoria's satisfaction. This measure would have hit South Africa far harder than the ban on the import of steel (imports of coal from South Africa amount to about $1.2 billion annually). Britain had let it be known that it would go along with a decision of the European Community to ban the import of coal, but the opposition of the Federal Republic (backed by Portugal), which can hardly have come as a surprise to London, proved insuperable. Foreign Minister Genscher argued that these measures would hit the South African mine workers hard and that the American administration was also opposed to coal sanctions.[26]

Shortly after this, in October 1986 the United States Congress, overriding a veto of President Reagan, adopted the Comprehensive Anti-Apartheid Act. This prohibited the import of coal, iron, steel, uranium, textiles, arms, ammunition, military vehicles, agricultural products, and food from South Africa and banned the export of all crude oil and petroleum products and of material for use in nuclear power plants. Moreover, exports of computers and related goods and services to the police, military and apartheid-enforcing entities were banned. New investment in South Africa was also banned, with few exceptions, and landing rights in the United States for South African aircraft were terminated.

This package of measures went far beyond the steps agreed upon by the European Community. The act also contained provisions for lifting or limiting sanctions if South African policy changed—provisions hardly likely to be used in the near future. The Act required the U.S. president to submit an annual report on the state of apartheid in South Africa and at the same time offer proposals for additional sanctions if "significant progress" toward ending apartheid had not been made. Although no progress was made in the first year after the bill was adopted, the president declined to propose new measures.

The fact that South Africa Minister for Foreign Affairs Roelof "Pik" Botha went as far as phoning individual U.S. senators to persuade them to vote against the act—with hints of South African countermeasures to the detriment of American farmers—shows how much importance Pretoria attached to the sanctions. However, any psychological effect of the sanctions on South African whites undoubtedly was weakened when the United States and Britain vetoed a 1987 UN Security Council resolution aimed at introducing mandatory sanctions comparable to those of the American Comprehensive Anti-Apartheid Act. In any case, Pretoria is not convinced that the position of Congress has moved the American Administration to any real change of course in its policy toward South Africa. In August 1987 Neil P. van Heerden, director-general of the South African Department of Foreign Affairs, declared that he did not believe there had been a fundamental change in Washington's policy toward Pretoria.[27]

It is also worth mentioning the general trade embargo against South Africa agreed to by the Scandinavian countries, whose trade with South Africa never was extensive, and the bans on the import of coal, iron, and steel imposed by Australian and Canada. Like the United States, Australia and Japan have decided to terminate landing rights for South African aircraft, and the Scandinavian countries have terminated commercial air services to South Africa. Zambia and Zimbabwe, on the other hand, vulnerable as they are to South Africa countermeasures, have so far not made any moves to terminate the landing rights of South African planes, although they had called for such a step in the London conference of the Commonwealth countries in August 1986.

Is it likely that the Western countries will take further steps in the coming years to increase economic pressure on South Africa? In the 1987 Commonwealth summit, Mrs. Thatcher again refused to bow to pressure for further sanctions. And in the European Community, she continues to find the German Chancellor, Helmut Kohl, at her side in her opposition to more far reaching steps. For both leaders it would, however, be much more difficult to maintain their resistance if events in South Africa took another turn for the worse. This would also be the case if Mr. Reagan's successor, instead of reluctantly carrying out the sanctions policy imposed by Congress, took the lead and urge allied countries to bring their sanctions more in line with those provided for in the Comprehensive Anti-Apartheid Act.

In South Africa itself there have been many calculations of the effects of sanctions. One interesting estimate was made by the Federated Chamber of industries in South Africa; it reckoned that all sanctions decided upon by the end of 1986 (no significant new ones were added during 1987) would reduce economic growth by 5 to 6 percent between 1987 and 1992. The total net effect might be a reduction of GDP and employment of the order of 4 percent.[28]

All studies suggest that the sanctions so far applied, though damaging to the South African economy, are not so catastrophic that South Africa will be forced to change course. The rapidly diminishing confidence of foreign banks and international companies in the future of South Africa, and the corresponding drop of new foreign investments and loans, was probably the worst blow South Africa received in recent years.

Undoubtedly the exodus of foreign companies from South Africa in 1986 and 1987 had the short-term effect that South African buyers were able to make large profits. But experts in South Africa do realize the adverse effects. Dr. Gerhard de Kock, the president of the Central Bank of South Africa, expressed the fear that the consequences would be financial isolation, the loss of trade connections and South Africa's falling behind in terms of technological development.[29] The technological effects might, however, be less than he assumes, since foreign investors who sell out also agree to contracts for the delivery of licenses and patents.

Can Sanctions Be Effective?

In recent years the allies have debated whether sanctions, if applied more fully than at present, could be successful in forcing Pretoria to abandon apartheid and to accept the legitimate role of the black majority in state and society. Theoretically, Pretoria could be checkmated quickly by a general trade embargo, coupled with a blockade of South African ports. However, apart from the Scandinavian countries, very few states have indicated a willingness to consider such a drastic step. In 1987, when the Security Council voted on a resolution proposing the breaking of all trade relations with South Africa as a punishment for its continuing illegal occupation of Namibia, three of South Africa's principal trading partners—the United States, Britain, and the Federal Republic—voted against, while Japan, France, and Italy abstained. The prospects of a naval blockade by the Western countries or by the UN seem even more remote.

Even without a general trade embargo, however, South Africa could be dealt a severe blow if the import of gold from South Africa were halted. (Gold makes up more than 40 percent of South Africa's total export earnings). If such an embargo were thus made effective, it would, however, lead to a rise in the price of gold—a development from which the Soviet Union, as a major gold producer, would profit most.[30] It seems improbable that the United States, for example, would be prepared to concede this advantage to the Soviet Union.

What, then, about Western measures to depress the price of gold and so increase the economic pressure on South Africa by decreasing its export earnings? There are also objections to this proposal. Other gold producers would also suffer—apart from the Soviet Union, mainly Brazil, Ghana, and Zambia. In addition, gold plays a role as security for the external debts of a number of countries. For these reasons, it seems unlikely that such a policy will be agreed to. Considering the damaging effects on the Western economies, it seems equally unlikely that agreement will be reached to halt the supply of minerals from South Africa.

Finally, South Africa has had many years to prepare for sanctions. For instance, it has undertaken large scale conversion of coal to oil and now meets half its petroleum needs this way.[31] Wherever possible, it has stockpiled those goods that might become scarce as a result of sanctions. South Africa, like Rhodesia in previous years, will be able to devise methods to make it appear that its textile and its agricultural products are not of South African origin.

Thus, the conclusion is inescapable that, while in theory various measures can be envisaged to have rapid and far reaching effects on the South African economy, these steps would in practice meet such serious objections as to preclude their acceptance. Moreover, the possibilities Pretoria has to weaken the impact of a number of sanctions must not be underestimated. Even if the governments in Washington, London, and Bonn could in principle recognize the need for stronger sanctions, it would be an illusion to think that such a program would leave Pretoria no other choice than to agree rapidly to Western demands for a fundamental change of its policies.

However, while *rapid* success for a sanctions policy is too much to expect, this does not mean that sanctions cannot play an important role in the struggle against the system of repression in South Africa. Apart from the economic damage caused by the modest sanctions agreed upon so far, there are the psychological effects on the white population. Sanctions convey the message that not only are they engaged in a dangerous confrontation with the black majority within South Africa, but they are also entering into a confrontation with the Western world to which they want so much to belong. Inevitably, their feeling of isolation must grow. The growing number of those who want to emigrate makes it clear that those are in the wrong who think that more pressure inevitably leads the laager to cling together even more strongly.

The psychological effects would be strengthened if the United States, the twelve member states of the European Community, Japan, and Canada could agree on a concerted and strong program of sanctions. The economic effects of sanctions could be considerably enhanced too. The United States, the European Community, and Japan together account for about two-thirds of total imports (excluding gold) from and about four-fifths of the exports (excluding oil) to South Africa.

In general, when deciding on policies toward South Africa, the allies should pay much more attention to psychological effects. For instance, everything possible should be done to secure the success of the boycott on sports contacts, which the Commonwealth conference at Gleneagles proposed as early as 1977. What has been done so far has had a great psychological impact, as is demonstrated by the remarkable attention given in South Africa to any successful attempt to break the boycott. A similar effect could be achieved if all Western countries followed the example of the United States (and a few other countries) and severed their air links with South Africa. It is also worth considering the withdrawal of all consular services from South Africa as was suggested by the Commonwealth conferences in 1985 and 1986. On the other hand, it would be unwise to break off all diplomatic relations, for without foreign embassies in South Africa, it would be much more difficult to monitor developments or to maintain contacts with black leaders and with those whites who realize the need for fundamental change.

Sanctions, though vital, should be only one part of a coordinated Western program to promote radical reforms in South Africa. Western policies must not simply exert pressure; they must also hold out to the whites in South Africa the prospect of cooperation instead of confrontation if they declare themselves ready to give up the politics of white supremacy. The major industrialized countries—the United States, Canada, the twelve EEC countries and Japan—could hold out the prospect of a large-scale program of aid, conditional on South Africa's breaking with apartheid. This two-track policy—making it clear to the whites that the present drift towards complete isolation is leading to ever greater sacrifices and eventually total disaster while offering them new prospects in the case of a radical change of direction—offers a greater hope of success than negative measures alone.

In order for this kind of message to be heard to best effect throughout South Africa, it should be proclaimed at the highest level, perhaps at the annual summit of the seven highly industrialized nations (the United States, Japan, Canada, the Federal Republic, France, Italy, and the United Kingdom) and, in the case of Europe, by the European Council—the heads of state or government of the twelve member states of the EEC. It should be crystal clear that the switch from sanctions to aid would not be triggered by vague promises or marginal concessions. But the Western countries should declare their willingness to suspend sanctions if Pretoria agreed to certain concrete steps: freeing Nelson Mandela and other black political leaders; unbanning the ANC and the PAC; ending the State of Emergency; and opening a dialogue with the released black leaders, who in turn would have to agree to suspend violence. The aid program should, however, start only when agreement has been reached on the structure of a post-apartheid South Africa.

Within the European Community, the Dutch minister for foreign affairs made a strong effort in 1987 to get a declaration of principles accepted by the other member states. But though there seemed to be general acceptance of the *contents* of the draft, the principle of issuing such a declaration was rejected by Britain and Portugal as counterproductive in South Africa. A somewhat similar proposal was made by Secretary of State Shultz during the Venice summit of the seven highly industrialized nations, but Mrs. Thatcher again made it clear that she was not prepared to accept it.

There is less reason to be pessimistic about the political feasibility of the idea of a conditional offer of aid to South Africa. The American Congress, as evidenced by Section 106(d) of the Comprehensive Anti-Apartheid Act, supports aid for South Africa provided it agrees to the abolition of apartheid. Within the European Community too, there is discussion of how to build positive elements into policy toward South Africa.

To be sure the solemn proclamation at a summit meeting of the sort of two-track policy advocated here would not immediately bring the walls of Botha's Jericho tumbling down. It would, however, bring the moment nearer when a majority of the whites will accept the inevitability of a radical change of policy. At the same time, the countries of the West should leave South Africa in no doubt that a further hardening of repression or new acts of aggression against neighboring states would lead to more far-reaching economic pressure. For instance, the present American and British policy of vetoing any draft resolution in the Security Council aimed at imposing mandatory sanctions against South Africa might be ended, a change of policy consistent in view of Section 401(e) of the Comprehensive Anti-Apartheid Act.[32]

If fundamental changes did take place in South Africa's political system, the Western countries would need a majority in the Security Council (and, at least, the abstention of the Soviet Union and China) to lift sanctions. Such cooperation might not be forthcoming. Moreover, sanctions would also have to applied by the Front Line States, raising the risk of South African countermeasures against them. Neither of these objections, however, seems insuperable. With veto power, the United States, Britain, and France would be in a strong negotiating position to insist on sanctions with provisions for their suspension. As for the Front Line States; mandatory sanctions would not necessarily trigger South African retaliation. For instance, the role of the Front Line States in implementing a mandatory ban on the export of oil or high technology products to South Africa would be minor.

In this context, South Africa can do itself harm by resorting to economic retaliation against neighboring states. South African exports to the countries of the Southern African Development Coordination Conference (Angola, Botswana, Lesotho, Malawi, Mozambique, Swaziland, Tanzania, Zambia, and Zimbabwe) amount to more than its total exports to the European Community of all food, agricultural, and coal products. The net freight revenue from the SADCC countries is estimated to be between $200 and $300 million annually. Invisible earnings, such as payment of dividends and profits of companies operating in the SADCC, energy purchases and pension remittances, especially from Zimbabwe, provide revenue of the same order of magnitude. Thus, "South Africa has an important long term interest in not retaliating within the region against sanctions imposed internationally."[33]

Western policy should not be limited to sanctions. Unofficial contacts between blacks and whites, as in July 1987 in Dakar; the black trade union movement COSATU; training and education of young blacks; aid to victims of apartheid: all these efforts deserve Western support. Support is necessary even if the South African government impedes such programs, a threat made in Botha's statement in the South African Parliament in August 1987: he viewed "in a very serious light the interference of foreign governments and their embassy personnel in the furtherance of extra parliamentary politics."[34] He also threatened to restrict the movements of certain staff members of specific embassies.

The West, Namibia and Angola

South Africa has been particularly intransigent over Namibia. Since 1966, when the General Assembly of the United Nations ended the mandate originally given to the country by the League of Nations, South Africa has continued its occupation of Namibia, notwithstanding the decision of the International Court and resolutions by the UN. In 1978 the so-called Western Contact Group—the United States, Britain, Canada, the Federal Republic and France—offered a plan for Namibian independence. Accepted by the UN as Resolution 435, the plan induced Pretoria to hold so-called "internal" elections in Namibia. Thereafter, however, South Africa raised all sorts of objections to the election provided for in Resolution 435, the proposed international supervision of the elections, and the size and composition of the United Nations Transition Assistance Group (UNTAG) that was to be set up. When by 1982 these problems too had finally been ironed out, South Africa linked its withdrawal to the withdrawal from Angola of Cuban troops that had arrived to help the MPLA government in Luanda in its struggle against the resistance movement UNITA. The United States took a similar position. Thus the questions of Namibia and Angola, where the South African forces frequently intervened to help UNITA, became inextricably linked.

There are clear differences between the policies of the United States and those of the European governments especially with regard to Angola. The United States does not recognize the Angolan government in Luanda, and in 1985 decided to supply arms to the resistance movement UNITA. The European states have diplomatic relations with the Luanda government and have distanced themselves from the aid given to UNITA. Moreover, they allowed Angola in 1985 to join the Lomé convention associating most African and Caribbean states with the European Community to provide Community aid and promote trade.

American anxiety about the presence of Cuban troops in Angola is understandable, but to most Europeans, American support for UNITA serves only to increase the Luanda regime's dependence on arms supplies from the communist world. In addition, American aid to UNITA, which receives strong support from South Africa, raises doubts in the rest of Africa about the credibility of the U.S. stand against apartheid. The same doubts exist for the whites of South Africa, to the detriment of attempts to convince them of the need for radical reform.

In January 1988 an American delegation led by Assistant Secretary of State, Chester Crocker, held negotiations in Luanda in which a Cuban delegation participated briefly, and in which Angolan and Cuban officials accepted for the first time the principle of withdrawing *all* Cuban troops (their number is estimated to be 40,000) from Angola in the context of a settlement. Differences remain, however, over the time frame for such a withdrawal, with the Americans maintaining that it should be as close as possible to the implementation of 435 and the independence of Namibia.

However, the South African government has reacted negatively to this development. Foreign Minister Botha said that Cuban forces would have to leave Angola before South Africa could start organizing elections in Namibia, and Pretoria also made it clear that no regional solution could be achieved without talks between all parties, including both UNITA and the Namibian government installed in Windhoek by South Africa. These reactions only strengthen the suspicion that South Africa is not genuinely interested in a settlement involving Cuban withdrawal from Angola and the independence of Namibia. It clearly prefers the present situation, which enables its forces to remain in both Namibia and southern Angola.

The West has an interest in seeing the Cubans disappear from Angola but not in supporting South Africa's policies toward Namibia and Angola. On the contrary as long as South Africa blocks a settlement, the Cubans will stay on in Angola. On the positive side, the government in Luanda should realize that the chances for a normalization of its relations with Washington would be considerably enhanced if it made further concessions on the timing of a Cuban withdrawal.

It would help if American policies toward UNITA and the MPLA government in Luanda were more in line with those of the European states. Ending American assistance to UNITA would end hopes in Pretoria, that, notwithstanding the Comprehensive Anti-Apartheid Act, American policies toward South Africa have not really changed. American aid for UNITA was inspired by fears of a victory by an MPLA perceived to be a tool in the hands of Moscow and Havana. Yet, signs point to a growing realization by the government in Luanda that it can only hope to revive its war ravished economy by establishing closer ties with the West.

For years, South Africa has occupied a position of secondary importance in the foreign policies of most Western countries. This cannot continue. Developments in South Africa threaten to end in a catastrophe whose effects will not be limited to that country alone or even to the region in which it is situated. Divisions within the Western world or halfhearted steps can only increase this danger. Efforts to develop a resolute, well-coordinated Western policy on South Africa deserves to have a high priority on the agendas of Western leaders. The United States in particular has a key role to play.

Despite the façade of inflexibility in South Africa, there are signs of self-doubt in the laager. A two-track Western policy—imposing sanctions so long as Pretoria refuses to make substantial reforms with sanctions, but encouraging those reforms with the conditional offer of a helping hand—might help, at the last moment, to avert the disaster that seems to be so near.

Notes

1. U.S. Department of State, Bureau of Public Affairs, *Current Policy* n.898.
2. U.S. Department of State, Bureau of Public Affairs, *Current Policy* n.853.
3. *NRC*/Handelsblad, Rotterdam, May 9, 1987.
4. *International Herald Tribune*, April 9, 1987.
5. *NRC*/Handelsblad, Rotterdam, May 9, 1987.
6. *International Herald Tribune*, December 9, 1987.
7. *NRC*/Handelsblad, Rotterdam, February 10, 1988.
8. Robert S. Jasser, "South Africa and its Neighbors; Dynamics of Regional Conflict," IISS *Adelphi papers*, 209, p.69 (summer 1986).
9. U.S. Department of State, Bureau of Public Affairs, *Current Policy* n.853.
10. *International Herald Tribune*, October 3, 1987.
11. *Volkskrant*, Amsterdam, February 17, 1988
12. U.S. Department of State, Bureau of Public Affairs, *Current Policy* n.853.

13. Speech in a debate on South Africa in the Bundestag, June 19, 1986.
14. Thomas G. Karis, "South Africa Liberation: The Communist Factor," *Foreign Affairs,* Winter 1986/1987, p. 282.
15. *International Herald Tribune,* July 13, 1987.
16. Cited in "A U.S. Policy Toward South Africa: The Report of the Secretary of State's Advisory Committee on South Africa," January 1987.
17. *Foreign Affairs,* Fall 1986, p.158.
18. Data on these and other minerals, provided by the U.S. Bureau of Mines, are included in the report of the Secretary of State's Advisory Committee on South Africa, "A U.S. Policy Toward South Africa," p.14.
19. J.P. Hayes, 'Economic Effects of Sanctions on South Africa", Trade Policy Research Centre, London 1987, p.70.
20. Ibid, p. 71.
21. "A U.S. Policy Toward South Africa," p. 3.
22. Hanns W. Maul, "South Africa's Minerals—The Achilles Heel of Western European Economic Security?," *International Affairs* 1986, p. 625/626.
23. *New York Times,* June 15, 1986.
24. U.S. Department of State, Bureau of Public Affairs, *Current Policy* n.853.
25. *Nation,* November 1986, p. 563.
26. *New York Times,* September 16, 1986.
27. *International Herald Tribune,* August 10, 1987.
28. Hayes, *Economic Effects of Sanctions,* p. 35.
29. *NRC*/Handelsblad, Rotterdam, July 8, 1987.
30. Charles M. Becker, "Economic Sanctions Against South Africa," *World Politics,* January 1987, p.157.
31. *Nation,* November 1986, p. 563.
32. Sec. 401(e) reads: It is the sense of the Congress that the President shall instruct the Permanent Representative of the United States to the United Nations to propose that the United Nations Security Council pursuant to Article 41 of the United Nations Charter, impose measures against South Africa of the same type as are imposed by this Act.
33. "Sanctions and South Africa's Neighbors," London May 1987, p.3.
34. *International Herald Tribune,* August 15, 1987.

Let Information Flow:
A Western Approach to
South Africa beyond Sanctions

Claude Cheysson

Violence in South Africa naturally provokes counterviolence; it gives birth to anxiety, fear, mutual mistrust, and this in turn seems to justify self defense, isolation, discrimination, a dreadful natural development applying to both sides. South Africa is thus leading to anarchy after a period that will see totalitarian force abused by both sides of the conflict.

The Sorry Record

Yet what has been tried and done by opponents of apartheid in South Africa and by Western countries has had a very limited impact. There have been many declarations, demonstrations, strikes, and protests, often made with great courage and determination. They have had little effect however, and sometimes even have given additional motivation to those who plead for violence and blood. In the world, moral condemnation has been expressed time and again. It has been a relief for those who expressed it; it has been an encouragement for those people who resist in South Africa. But one must be realistic and admit that it has not been taken as significant by the present leadership of South Africa.

A large number of international conventions denounce racial discrimination, discrimination in employment, discrimination in education; they have laid down procedures for the settlement of disputes, opened possibilities of recourse to international courts. But who in South Africa was really impressed by this United Nations legal architecture? Campaigns then excluded South Africa from many international organizations. I dispute the wisdom of such an approach. Removing a culprit from the

competence of those who should condemn his sins runs against
the very purpose of the measure in the first place, just as a
decision to severe diplomatic relations by the Western countries
that disagree with apartheid policies would relieve South Africa
from direct pressures.

In brief, in the political field, in our countries, domestically as
well as beyond, we must accept that what has been done has not
changed much in southern Africa.

Have economic actions been more effective? Sanctions by
foreign countries have been proposed, and some have actually
been put in force. At long last, something was thus done; moral
condemnation of South Africa was taking a concrete expression,
and this deserves attention. But let us also be realistic and assess
the real impact:

In the armament field, sanctions were decided by the UN
Security Council—the body competent, according to the Charter, to make compulsory decisions and impose them. The ban
has been and is effective to a point, namely for the supply of
sophisticated equipment. However, previous such decisions
have proved to stimulate imaginations and bypasses; the final
beneficiaries are the intermediaries whose profit increases in
proportion to the obstacles. Furthermore, the ban has given a
remarkable boost to the South African armament industry; even
in the nuclear field, South Africa seems to have progressed and
found suppliers. (In my previous job, I happen to have known
precisely of a supply of Chinese heavy water to South Africa.)

Who could say that the main problem of the South African
authorities in the pursuance of the apartheid policy is a shortage
of such arms?

Beyond armaments, economic sanctions do not seem promis-
ing:

- To try and cut South Africa from essential imports is a
  hopeless exercise, even if it were made compulsory by the
  Security Council for all countries in the world;
- To ban export of minerals and other commodities from
  South Africa would be detrimental to Western countries for
  some raw materials; therefore a large part of such exports

would find their way to industrialized markets, probably
through third countries and other intermediaries;
- The withdrawal of foreign investment would be a double-
edged sword, as in the early stage, South African companies
would derive benefits from the purchase of equipment and
plants at cheap prices even if such companies later had
difficulties with access to advanced technology;
- A prohibition of new investment is probably the most
damaging measure for the South African economy, as was
illustrated by the fall of the rand when a number of
American enterprises published their decision to withdraw.
But it would only be impressive if it were applied by all,
which is far from the case.

In discussing economic sanctions, South African leaders and
their supporters in Europe highlight the implications for workers
in the black community—decreases in revenue and unemployment. Yet it is noteworthy that this argument is not used by the
leaders of the black community, even by moderates (the
Southern African Catholic Bishops, for example). On the
contrary, they stress that a fundamental change in the society is
bound to provoke sufferings for the mass of the people, but they
accept it if it means change.

In conclusion, as economic sanctions have now become a
symbol, it is politically necessary to build them up progressively.
The UN Security Council should adopt them as provided for by
the Charter. Economic sanctions would thus become part of the
world system of law, compulsory for all. The new authority of
the UN Security Council resulting from the recent change of
attitude of the Soviets under Gorbachev would give additional
psychological impact to such a decision. Still, we must admit
that none of the measures and declarations considered above
will fundamentally change the actual situation in South Africa.
We have to accept that none will bring South Africa to its knees.

What Can Be Done?

1. Certainly we must help the anti-apartheid communities in
South Africa to survive, to develop, and to keep their identity.

We must support the policies of responsible moderate leaders in their constructive approaches. As one says in French, *"il ne faut pas insulter l'avenir"* (we must not insult the future). A constant relationship with such leaders is therefore essential, not only to be well informed of the actual situation, but also to confirm their authority—in itself a protection against some abuse by the police, intelligence services, and local authorities. This support should be given within and outside South Africa.

Within South Africa, our embassies, companies, and institutions should seize every occasion to apply nondiscriminatory policies, to express views, and make demarches, even to give asylum: the Dutch Embassy did so recently, and a few years ago a French ambassador saved the life of Breyton Breytenbach when he intervened immediately after the latter's arrest. I also favor visits to South Africa by personalities whose presence and statements will be publicized—Senator Edward Kennedy's visit in 1986 was widely reported.

It is important that direct support be made available to South African nongovernmental organizations (NGOs)—councils of churches, trade unions, educational bodies—whose actions relieve suffering, give special attention to political prisoners and their families, and exchange information. The European Community has voted special credits for such support, now at a level of some $25 million per year, an amount that could be increased. Some European NGOs—for example, "Médecins du monde"— have managed to work in and for the benefit of black communities, often at great personal risk.

Outside South Africa, television and radio networks that can reach South Africa should be used more widely to give information, pass messages, and express protests. I remember a speech I delivered in Maseru, Lesotho, years ago; it had a certain impact in the two big cities of Pretoria and Johannesburg where it was reported live by TV and radio.

Invitations for visits abroad will have a similar effect on the morale and authority of the moderate leaders. We now receive in Brussels and Strasbourg a reasonably large number of leaders, white and black, representing churches, trade unions, and humanitarian institutions. They come from South Africa, and also from Namibia. They are also invited to international meetings where they can give information, bear witness, and receive encouragement that they will then bring back home.

So, too, every occasion should be used to give scholarships and fellowships to students and educators. The apartheid policies tend to isolate; we should systematically try to break the isolation.

2. As all chapters in this book stress, developments in South Africa are bound to affect South Africa's trade partners. Therefore, we must try to limit the effects and close windows of vulnerability. As far as the industrialized countries are concerned, this means diversifying supply sources of the few raw materials for which we are still heavily dependent on South Africa: chromium, platinum, vanadium. We must also limit as much as possible our imports of coal and uranium ore, and there are many other countries where such minerals can be found.

Much more important is assistance to neighboring sovereign African states to help them become less dependent on South Africa. This will be difficult and costly, as dependence is heavy in three fields: employment, communication, and exports. In the first two, a large program of national and regional development is needed for landlocked states and for Mozambique and Swaziland; Namibia will have a similar need after independence. As for exports, preference should be given for entry into our markets to the products of South Africa's six neighbors that are now exported mainly to South Africa; this applies more particularly to products of Zimbabwe. A significant part of such exports are agricultural commodities; access to European and American markets will therefore be difficult to improve.

However, we must understand that the success of multiracial societies at the doors of South Africa would have a deep effect on mentalities in every quarter in South Africa. No effort should be spared, for this is far more important than critical speeches on Sunday, fiery declarations of intent and timid measures addressed directly at Pretoria.

3. A success story in Namibia would have the most dramatic impact, and it should be possible to make it happen. The economic potential of Namibia is diverse and rich; its harbor

facilities, coasts, and sea resources are remarkable assets. Among its people, there is a white Namibian community, partly of German descent, already committed to independence; a few I know are even members of the nationalist movement SWAPO and take part in the struggle for independence. They are ready to assume responsibilities in an independent Namibia.

International aid is likely to be available to Namibia immediately after independence, as the United Nations has already taken a formal decision by Resolution 435 to make South African occupation illegal. Substantial assistance can be expected from Western European states, and especially the European Community, which supports the efforts of all independent countries south of the Sahara through the Lomé Convention. One of our member states, the Federal Republic, feels particularly concerned because of historical and cultural ties with the territory and part of the people.

Pressure should thus be increased on Pretoria for an early and full observance of UN Resolution 435. In this regard, it is highly desirable that the position of the United States should be less ambiguous. The Department of State, in particular, should be convinced that unity of expression by Western countries is essential. Ambiguity does not help South Africa in the long run, and the very serious problems in Angola should be dealt with on their own merits.

If the U.S. government is, in my opinion, at times too shy in its attitude, too preoccupied with keeping a decent relation with Pretoria, this in itself is not dangerous because of the continued pressure of American public opinion. All Americans resent deeply any discrimination based on the color of the skin. The pressure against apartheid will therefore keep on increasing. No one in Europe should have any doubt about it.

Many will object that Pretoria has decided to refuse any move toward real independence of former South West Africa. However, should public pressure increase, and as those presently responsible for the apartheid policy cannot make substantial concessions at home, there is a chance of a change of attitude about Namibia. That territory, after all, can pose no direct threat because of the large stretch of desert separating it from the densely populated areas in South Africa—Maputo, Mozambique is much closer than Windhoek.

4. In 1957 I became the Secretary General of an international organization dealing with technical cooperation in Africa south of the Sahara (CCTA). The six founder members were four colonial powers (Belgium, France, Portugal, and Britain) and two white African states (South Africa and the then "Federation of Rhodesia and Nyasaland"). When Ghana joined in 1957, immediately after its independence, Kwame Nkrumah—who did not yet act as a prophet—advised me to arrange as many meetings as possible in South Africa, or with good South African experts and scientists. It was important, he said, that they should know more of the capacities of other Africans, of African economies and institutions.

A few years later and after a number of newly independent black African states had joined CCTA, a white Boer, good friend of mine, a psychiatrist of repute, resigned from all his official positions in Pretoria and in the universities because, he told me, he had "discovered, in meeting with colleagues coming from the rest of Africa to attend CCTA conferences, that the blacks could be as learned, articulate, and effective as any white." His previous assessment of their capacities had proved to be entirely wrong, and, "in his conscience," he could not support any more the apartheid policy that until then in his mind had been justified by the belief of a natural, genetic inferiority of the blacks. He had believed that it was the will of God that the sons of Cham be inferior to the sons of Sem; he knew now that he was wrong, and it changed his life.

A few months later, Verwoerd, then prime minister of South Africa, let me know that his country would withdraw from my inter-African organization, because, he said, South African scientists, experts, professors tended to gain in our meetings the "illusion that blacks could equal whites." He used almost the same expressions as my psychiatrist friend, but with opposite conclusions.

Why Tell This Story?

I tell this story because I am convinced that a large number of the Boers who support apartheid are, or have been, sincere. They are, or have been, convinced that it was a duty for the whites to educate the blacks, to look after their health and living conditions, to isolate them from the contagion of disorder, anarchy, mismanagement, and incompetence that prevails elsewhere in Africa. And they are proud of some material achievements in this regard.

I therefore recommend that information flow into South Africa. At all levels, in particular among the educated people and the young, there should be a better knowledge of who "the others" really are, what they can do, what fundamental rights all human beings have—not only to keep different colors of skin but also to keep their cultures and their identities.

Borders of South Africa should be reopened and kept open; as many young people as possible—namely white young people—should travel abroad, in our countries and in Africa. They should have a chance to study, to work, to live, to play sports, among friends in our cities and universities. In South Africa itself they should be induced to receive as many friends of their age, colleagues of their specialty, partners of their sport as possible.

It is essential that indisputable personalities of authority should tell them, warn them, even shame them: how can a good Christian ignore the teachings of Christ? How can a man who believes in God, who asserts that every man has the right to be respected, how can he accept that another man should be discriminated against for the simple reason that his skin is not white? The yellow star did not justify the treatment imposed to the Jews by the Nazis; the black skin does not either.

Most of the Boers are good Christians and practice their religion; they have a clear conscience because they are convinced that they are on earth to fulfill a mission, in full respect of the will of God. Give them a bad conscience when a black suffers injury. Let them count as sin every discrimination against another son of God, be he black or white.

Conveying this message is, first and foremost, the responsibility of respected authorities—bishops, Nobel Prize winners. A Gandhi has done more than many resolutions of obscure international committees, and a Macmillan had a greater impact with his famous speech on the "Wind of Change." Domestically, a black bishop is more influential and important than a hundred angry demonstrators.

I know that my approach will surprise many, possibly a great majority of those who will read these lines. I have put in question the reality and effectiveness of most economic sanctions—although without disputing their moral effect. I have expressed doubts about the wisdom of withdrawing foreign diplomats, banning direct relations, and I have even recommended that relations of all types should be multiplied, diversified, and extended.

I have expressed such views because I sincerely believe that there is no evil in the ordinary man. I am convinced that most of the supporters of apartheid are misinformed, that they live on basic misconceptions. Everything should be undertaken to change such concepts and to remove barriers. We all agree that there must be multiracial universities—one of the first significant decisions of the apartheid government was to break the multiracial character of the Witwatersrand University. We all think that "petty apartheid" must be ended in buses, on benches in the street, in hotels, and cinemas. Why not take the same approach to relations between all South Africans, including all whites, and the rest of the world; between white men in the white streets of South Africa and men in the streets of black Africa, Europe, America?

Forging a Western Consensus on South Africa

Herman W. Nickel

South Africa is now discussed in the West largely in terms of ending the evil of apartheid and the instability it causes within South Africa and between the country and its neighbors. But whether the end of apartheid also resolves the crisis of southern Africa depends crucially on how it passes, and what succeeds it. These are the critical and inseparable questions that any responsible Western anti-apartheid strategy will have to address.

The Primacy of Domestic Politics

What distinguishes the South African issue from most other foreign policy problems is that it is emotionally potent, with important domestic constituencies that force governments and politicians to deal with the issue in these terms as well. Reconciling foreign policy concerns with domestic political requirements and crafting sound policies that can be sustained politically will continue to remain a vexing task for Western governments.

This is especially critical in the United States where, for better or worse, Congress has effectively asserted its coequal role in foreign policy vis-à-vis the presidency, and even local and state governments have become active on this foreign policy issue (thus far without any constitutional challenge from the federal government). It is in the nature of the political process that elected representatives will deal with the South African issue primarily as a constituency problem, and only secondarily in terms of the actual effects of their votes on the situation in South Africa itself. In their dealings with Washington, foreign governments have been put on notice that South Africa is among those foreign policy issues for which it cannot be assumed that the executive branch can make its writ run.

Harmonizing the policies of the members of the alliance poses an additional challenge. Without a coordination of policies and diplomatic initiatives, the West's ability to influence events in South Africa, already limited, will be further diminished. Blame-shifting and finger-pointing are bound to increase as policies fail to produce the desired, ambitious results or fail to produce them quickly enough to satisfy an impatient public.

The nature of American and Western European concerns in what happens in South and southern Africa has many common denominators. The denial of equal political and other basic human rights to the large majority of South Africans on the basis of their race is profoundly offensive to all democratic members of the alliance. Anti-apartheid movements exist in virtually all the countries of the alliance. But there are significant differences in intensity and mix. This inevitably complicates the task of developing common approaches and preventing the South African issue from becoming a growing source of strain within the alliance.

What gives the South African issue its very special character in the United States is that it has become an extension of the country's most sensitive domestic issue—race. As such, it touches the raw nerves of a body politic in which the ethos of racial equality continues, despite major gains, to collide with everyday reality. In their approach to the South African issue, many Americans are thus dealing less with perceived foreign policy interests than with how they like to feel about themselves and their country. Images of racial repression in South Africa that revive memories of Selma, Alabama, trigger a powerful combination of mutually reinforcing emotions, of black anger and white guilt. To point out this obvious fact in no way detracts from the validity of the moral case against apartheid.

The practical political impact of this phenomenon is greatest in the Democratic Party, which depends vitally on the support of the liberal and black constituencies. In these constituencies, opposition to apartheid has become synonymous with a strongly punitive approach. Anything less exposes a politician to the

charge of being "soft on racism," a charge as deadly as the
charge of being "soft on communism" ever was. Since the
cathartic symbolism matters more than the actual results, this
approach is likely to persist even when its actual effects may
turn out to be counterproductive in South Africa and destructive
to American influence there. If the initial sanctions succeed only
in making Pretoria more truculent, this will be taken as proof
that tougher sanctions are needed. If more positive developments take place—the defection of some liberal Afrikaners from
the National Party before the May 1987 white elections and the
meeting of some prominent Afrikaners with the ANC in Dakar,
also in 1987, were both treated in this way—it will be cited as
evidence that sanctions are working.

Only a serious and open split among prominent black leaders
over the wisdom of sanctions and disengagement would provide
liberal white politicians in the United States with the "cover" to
challenge the current orthodoxy that an anti-apartheid policy is
a sanctions policy. So far this has not happened, at least not out
in the open. But it may yet, especially as black South Africans
voice their disillusionment with the results of sanctions. For the
moment, peer pressure has similar inhibiting effects both in the
United States and South Africa.

The racial component is the dynamic that really "drives" the
South Africa issue in American politics, far more than any
economic, strategic or political considerations, none of which are
perceived as truly vital (in the sense of being worth going to war
for). To the extent that a similar dynamic exists in other alliance
countries—increasingly multiracial Britain probably comes closest—it is balanced by countervailing interests that, again, are
relatively more important to these countries than they are to the
United States. Efforts by the U.S. to force allied countries to fall
into line with its own anti-apartheid measures and to penalize
countries that "take commercial advantage" of them could thus
become serious irritants in the relations between America, its
NATO partners, and Japan.

For instance, provisions to impose trade penalities on countries taking advantage of U.S. sanctions against South Africa was
part of the Dellums-Cranston bill before Congress in 1988.

Another provision, introduced by Democratic Congressman Bob Wise from the coal-producing state of West Virginia, would exclude all foreign oil companies doing business in South Africa from federal land leases. If enacted, this would have serious repercussions for such companies as British Petroleum and Royal Dutch/Shell, both of which have major interests in North America. It could, conceivably, lead to pressure to retaliate against American oil companies seeking leases in such areas as the North Sea.

Foreign governments, on the whole, resent being pressured to sacrifice policy and commercial interests for the sake of placating domestic constituencies in the United States. An allied leader like Prime Minister Margaret Thatcher, who has rejected sanctions as fundamentally counterproductive of their stated objectives and has steadfastly maintained that position despite strong criticism from Commonwealth countries, is not likely to budge easily from her stand. Her stand reinforces the resistance of other European leaders who have expressed themselves less forcefully on the issue but essentially share her view.

Consequently, the more U.S. policy toward South Africa is perceived abroad as a function of American domestic politics, the greater reluctance there is likely to be to follow Washington's lead. To be sure, the relationship with the United States means much more to Washington's European and Japanese allies than does their relationship to South Africa, but the political price the United States would pay for an effort to impose its own will in this matter could be considerable—especially in the context of other strains in the relationship. Only common perceptions of foreign policy interests and a broad consensus on the best means of advancing and defending them can provide a sound basis for allied cooperation, on this as on other issues.

Differing Interests

To a much greater degree than the United States, European nations have traditionally seen themselves as dependent on trade. As a rule, this makes them skeptical of trade sanctions and embargoes, thus reluctant to follow American leadership. West German resistance to Washington's pressure to call off the pipeline deal with the Soviet Union is a case in point. For Britain and the Federal Republic, trade and investment ties with South Africa matter far more than they do to the United States. While South African trade represents less than 1 percent of total U.S. foreign trade and less than 1 percent of overseas investment, Britain's stake is much greater. In 1985 the income from sales of goods and services to South Africa plus earnings from investments was $5.9 billion, an amount exceeding the British government's revenues from North Sea oil. Estimates of the number of British jobs dependent on trade with South Africa go as high as 250,000. The Federal Republic is South Africa's biggest European trading partner and its biggest foreign supplier. Its trade with South Africa in 1985 came to $2.7 billion. Within the European Community, Italy comes third. France, in fourth place, has as a rule not allowed political considerations to stand in the way of trade. Dutch and Scandinavian trade with South Africa is not a significant factor that would seriously inhibit the inclination of these countries toward economic sanctions. In the case of Canada, which, like Australia, competes with South Africa's mining products, there is a positive economic interest in restricting South Africa's access to world markets.

Similar differences exist in the field of travel. The United States has no "kith and kin" ties with South Africa worth mentioning. Well before the Congress in October 1986 barred South African aircraft from landing in the United States, Pan American had quit the direct route from New York to Johannesburg for strictly economic reasons. By contrast, because of family and business ties, travel matters greatly for Britain, since as many as one million white South Africans can claim British passports. Seven hundred-and-fifty thousand Portuguese have settled in South Africa and retain dual citizenship, including the right to vote in Portuguese elections. To a lesser extent, such family ties are also a factor in Germany and the Netherlands.

With a strong Deutsche mark and a weak rand plus a subsiding of unrest, Germany's inveterate tourists have once again discovered that South Africa is a remarkable travel bargain, as have other Europeans. As a result the lucrative air routes to and from South Africa continue to be of major importance to European airlines. Any American effort to force the European airlines to suspend their South African services by threatening their landing rights in the U.S. would meet with fierce resistance.

In other areas, American and European interests and threat assessments are more compatible. All the members of the alliance have reason to be concerned about disruptions in the production and supply of key strategic minerals for which South Africa remains the most significant non-communist source. This will be true so long as adequate stockpiles do not exist and substitutes are either unavailable or too expensive. The critical minerals are the platinum group of metals now in short supply, chromium and ferrochrome, manganese and ferromanganese. Moreover, South Africa's extensive railroad network moves a large proportion of the mining production of Zaire (including strategically critical cobalt), Zambia, Zimbabwe, and Namibia. Increasing dependence on the other major producer of these items, the Soviet Union, would seem to be hard to justify on either strategic or human rights grounds, Gorbachev notwithstanding. There would, therefore, seem to be a basis for the members of the alliance to develop a common minerals strategy to safeguard against extended disruptions of supplies. So far, little if anything has been done along these lines.

At the same time, it stands to reason that any South African government, of whatever complexion will have an overriding interest in selling minerals wherever the market is—and effectively that means the non-communist Free World. Thus there is little merit to the converging arguments from far right and far left that the West should do the bidding of either present or future South African rulers, or risk losing the supply of these minerals. The real question is whether the minerals will be produced without prolonged disruptions and in adequate quantity.

Nor is there doubt that a disruption of the sea routes around the Cape of Good Hope would have critical effects on the members of the alliance. The 3,000 ships that round the Cape of Good Hope each year carry 90 percent of Western Europe's oil consumption, 70 percent of its strategic minerals, 20 percent of

U.S. oil imports, and 25 percent of Western Europe's food supply. What is doubtful is the seriousness of the threat. Other choke points, like the Straits of Hormuz, are far more obvious. As the report of the Secretary of State's Advisory Committee on South Africa put it in January, 1987, "the apparent consensus among U.S. defense planners is that these sea-lanes are under minimal threat and that the active collaboration of the South African government would not significantly increase our ability to protect them." What matters more is that South Africa should not fall under the control of a government that might allow the establishment of a Soviet military presence that would make such a threat more serious.

Such a presence would be disastrous for a post-apartheid South Africa itself, for it would seriously jeopardize the prospects of Western help. Notwithstanding their support of the African National Congress, the Soviets themselves appear to have little taste for assuming the major responsibilities that would follow in the wake of a successful revolution. A look at the Soviet Union's pitiful economic assistance record in nearby southern African countries like Mozambique and Angola should drive the point home.

Nor does Moscow seem to have any illusions that a fullscale revolution is at all imminent or even likely. For the time being they seem content to keep the South African pot simmering, but without having it boil over. Their approach may change, but the present Soviet leadership does not appear to have much enthusiasm for South African policies that are costly in terms of resources and U.S.-Soviet relations.

Scope for Negotiation

If the members of the alliance attach different weights to their stakes in southern Africa, the common denominator is that these interests are all jeopardized by the prospect of worsening instability—within South Africa itself and in relations between South Africa and the rest of the region. Instability is the consequence of an isolated and truculent white minority regime that, even as it continues its efforts to coopt blacks into its political and economic system, increasingly relies on repression of its internal foes and intimidation of its neighbors to keep itself in power. By the same token, however, the installation of a black revolutionary regime that hides its totalitarian reality behind the rhetoric of a majority would be equally incompatible with Western interests and values. Much as the West would like to see an end to the evils of apartheid, it has no interest in seeing one repressive and unfriendly regime replaced by another.

Clearly, the most desirable outcome worth striving for would be a political and constitutional accommodation that satisfied the basic aspirations and concerns of all the elements of South Africa's multiracial and multi-ethnic society and that effectively protected the rights of the individual and provided the basis for a vibrant economy that could meet the demands of a burgeoning population. Such an order cannot be imposed from without; only South Africans can create it. For better or for worse, however, the outside world can have an impact on the South African political process and atmosphere. Its influence would be for the worse if it strengthened the resolve of the extremes of the South African spectrum by encouraging black militants to hold out for illusory visions of total victory while on the other hand maximizing the existential fears of whites concerned about their future in a black ruled South Africa. It would be far better if the outside world lent support and encouragement to those elements working for peaceful solutions.

It is thus important for the alliance to signal clearly that its categorical rejection of apartheid and all its evils does not constitute support for revolutionary violence, and that, to paraphrase Martin Luther King, it will judge a post-apartheid government not by the color of those who run it but by the quality of its character. But mere calls for negotiations without indicating the substantive framework for a settlement soon tend to be dismissed by all sides as rituals, especially so long as the main antagonists take incompatible positions that rule out any progress toward agreement. In his New York speech of September 29, 1987, Secretary of State George Shultz for the first time spelled out the elements of a settlement which would meet the aspirations of the black majority, the concerns of whites and other minorities, and that the United States could support. He appealed for:

- A constitutional order establishing equal political economic and social rights for all South Africans;
- A democratic electoral system with multiparty participation and universal adult franchise;
- Effective constitutional guarantees of basic human rights for all South Africans as provided for in the Universal Declaration of Human Rights;
- The rule of law, safeguarded by an independent judiciary with the power to enforce rights guaranteed by the constitution to all South Africans;
- A constitutional allocation of powers between the national government and its constituent regional and local jurisdictions;
- An economic system that guarantees economic freedom, allocates governmental social and economic services fairly and enables all South Africans to realize the fruits of their labor, acquire and own property, and attain a decent standard of living.

Since these principles represent the democratic essentials that the alliance was formed to advance, the allies should embody them in a collective statement of principle, as a marker for what it would support in negotiations among South Africans themselves. The statement would serve as a useful antidote to delusions among black militants on the radical end of the spectrum that the West supports their revolutionary agenda, and to the view of many whites that the West is committed to black majority rule regardless of its moral and constitutional content. These perceptions are inimical to negotiations and a constructive Western role in facilitating that process. As U.S. Ambassador to South Africa Edward J. Perkins put it: "we can choose principles, we cannot choose sides."[1]

Looking at the present South African scene, the odds of reaching an agreement within the broad framework of the Shultz principles seem extremely small. Indeed, public discussion of the South African crisis in the West has for so long been dominated by forebodings of imminent cataclysm that the possibility of accommodation is often thought to have passed some time ago, leaving the West with little choice but to get on the "right"—or "winning"—side in the inevitable apocalyptic showdown. But that reading of the situation is wrong, and dangerously so. Far more likely is a period of prolonged stalemate in which no side can impose its will, accompanied by inconclusive, recurring cycles of violent protest and repression. Even as these collisions take place, however, the parties to the conflict will be forced to come to terms with one another's true strength. Developments in South African labor relations illustrate this pattern most clearly. As they demonstrated in the 1987 mine strike, the South African mining houses, however reluctantly, were prepared to exercise the ultimate power of dismissal, but the inescapable reality of a powerful black miners' union is one they know they cannot ignore.

Numbers alone will over time produce an ascendancy in black bargaining strength, as the differential in birth rates reduces the white minority from the current 15 percent to below 10 percent in the early 2000s. The economic clout of black consumers, workers, and entrepreneurs will also rise, though by how much will critically depend on the economic growth rate. (Of course, access to economic opportunity is another matter.) Mass unemployment damages black economic leverage since the unemployed cannot strike but can help break strikes, and have little consumer power to exercise. The somber reality is that the vigorous growth rate of 5 to 6 percent required to absorb 300,000 young blacks into the job market each year is precluded by the virtual end to capital inflows from abroad—the result not so much of formal sanctions as of doubts in the international financial community about South Africa's future stability. This sanction of the market—a far more flexible mechanism than sanctions imposed by politicians—has had the greatest economic impact thus far. The projected growth rate for 1988 is 3 percent, better than expected but still woefully short of what is needed to curb the scourge of black unemployment that is now running at 25 to 30 percent.

The South African economist R. W. Bethlehem forecasts that by the year 2000, given a 3 percent black birth rate, unemployment is likely to reach 43.8 percent without sanctions. With sanctions, he concludes that 55.1 percent would be a conservative estimate, a difference of about 2 million jobs.[2] With 54 percent of the black population (in 1980) under the age of 20, the sociopolitical implications of this inability of the economy to create sufficient employment could be explosive for any future government of South Africa, regardless of its political or racial complexion.

Yet if the historic tide is clearly running in favor of the black majority, the balance of power for the foreseeable future will not permit it to dictate terms to a determined and powerful white minority. This is especially true so long as the black majority remains plagued by deep divisions and tragic political blood feuds that the government can easily manipulate. By the same token, however, the minority regime cannot perpetuate its dominant position by repression.

For now, sadly, neither side seems disposed to negotiate: "Parties to a dispute begin negotiations when they have concluded that victory on their terms is not possible. The major parties in this particular conflict are the South African regime and the major resistance groupings. Significant elements in each continue to believe that they can 'win.' The regime continues to believe that it can coercively impose its notions of 'reform'; many in the resistance groupings think that a determined struggle will lead to the complete collapse of the apartheid regime. . . . As long as this cocky assurance marks the public postures of major actors in the South African drama, negotiations are a long way off."[3]

How much more suffering will the competing parties have to inflict on each other—and indeed on the entire region—before they finally realize that the costs of continued conflict exceed the costs of compromise? No one, certainly not the members of the Western alliance, can remain indifferent to the gloomy prospect of a key regional power coming to terms with itself only after destroying itself. It evokes the haunting phrase of Tacitus: ". . .they create a wasteland, and they call it peace."

What we can hope is that for all the conflict over who wields political power, there remains an underlying awareness of a fateful South African reality of multiracial interdependence that necessitates accommodation and cooperation. This coincidence of conflict and mutual dependence will continue to define the South African predicament.

The critical policy question before the members of the alliance is: what can and should be done to facilitate accommodation in South Africa? And, just as important, what would make the process more difficult? Surely, public pressure to "do something" does not absolve politicians and governments from the moral injunction of the Hippocratic oath, "above all, do no harm."

Patterns of Vulnerability

Fashioning an effective Western policy toward South Africa requires a realistic assessment of Western influence. Otherwise, by defining ambitious policy goals that exceed that actual degree of Western leverage, successive policies will be condemned to failure from the outset. Delusions of Western omnipotence flow from wishful thinking on the part of anti-apartheid campaigners both inside and outside South Africa: if only the West had the resolve, it also would have the power to "end apartheid" quickly. The most prominent black South African advocate for a policy of international isolation and sanctions abroad, Archbishop Desmond Tutu, has told American audiences on many occasions that "if only it wanted to" the United States could end the nightmare of apartheid "tomorrow."

The reverse side of this coin is that so long as the United States does not produce this liberating result, it must be because it is not really trying. Suspicions that the United States government cares more about the future fate of South African whites than it does about the present sufferings of the black majority blend easily with fanciful but nonetheless popular ideological notions that capitalist greed drives American policy. The belief that capitalism and apartheid are one and the same enemy is firmly ensconced in the rhetoric of such anti-apartheid labor leaders as Cyril Ramaphosa, the militant president of the National Union of Mineworkers.

If this thesis—coming from the victims of apartheid who desperately believe that outside pressure is the only alternative to the agony of protracted violence—is understandable, it still does not withstand serious critical scrutiny.

In fact, South Africa is probably less vulnerable to international economic pressures than most other countries. It is one of the few African countries that is self-sufficient in food. It is rich in mineral resources, on many of which the West critically depends. Gold and diamonds, which account for over 60 percent of the country's exports, are easily transported, their movements next to impossible to control. Coal provides the country with a rich energy base. Even the vulnerability with respect to petroleum has been dramatically reduced. Built up and maintained at huge cost, the government's strategic fuel reserve is a closely guarded secret. But enough crude oil is said to be stored away to support current normal levels of consumption for between three to five years. Coal liquefaction, though still more expensive than refining crude oil, covers one-third of the demand for gasoline. A major off-shore gas project is being developed off Mossel Bay. Given South Africa's long coastline, a strict oil embargo would require much more naval enforcement than the Royal Navy had to engage in patrolling the Mozambique Straits and access to the port of Beira during the period sanctions were in effect against the Smith regime in Rhodesia.

Finally, South Africa has developed a sophisticated industrial sector. In recent years it has received something of a windfall through the firesale of the assets and technology of major American multinational companies that left South Africa under political pressures at home. One of the unintended effects of the mandatory arms embargo imposed by the UN Security Council in 1977 has been to build up the South African arms industry to the point where it is now ranked as the tenth largest arms exporter. Despite weaknesses in supersonic fighters and transport aircraft, South Africa remains the regional superpower.

While South Africa itself is thus relatively immune to international sanctions, the most immediate victims would be its weaker neighbors. South Africa is the major trading partner of Botswana, Lesotho, and Swaziland, as well as Zimbabwe. It is the greatest source of imports for Mozambique and Malawi. Except for Tanzania, each of the members of the Southern African Development Coordination Conference (SADCC), which was formed to reduce dependence on South Africa, has more trade with South Africa than with all its SADCC partners combined, and total SADCC trade with South Africa is seven times higher than intra-SADCC trade."[4]

Possibly more critical is the continued dependence of the Front Line States on South Africa's efficient rail and harbor system to carry a substantial part of their exports and imports. During 1985–86, at least 45 percent of the aggregate total overseas goods traffic of Zimbabwe, Zambia, and Malawi were carried to and from South African ports by South African Transport Services. Whether efforts to reopen the Benguela Railroad through Angola, the Beira Corridor and the Chicuala-cuala-Maputo line, and Malawi's routes to Nacala and Beira will substantially reduce this dependence hinges on events on the ground in Mozambique and Angola. Zimbabwe still sends about 90 percent of its overseas goods traffic through South Africa; while it hopes that by 1990 Beira will be able to handle 90 percent of this traffic, the country would still be heavily dependent on South Africa. Zambia has succeeded in diverting its copper exports away from South African ports and channels them via both the Chinese-built Tazara railway to Dar es Salaam and the port of Beira. However, the bulk of Zambia's imports still come from or through South Africa. Botswana's dependence is even greater, and that of Lesotho, as a landlocked enclave within South Africa, total.

In the field of air transport, because of the long distances separating southern Africa from maintenance facilities in Europe and the United States, airlines Air Zimbabwe, Royal Swazi Air, Linhas Aereas de Mozambique, and Air Mauritius have used South African Airways maintenance and training facilities.

Finally, the remittances of migrant workers, mainly miners, who have traditionally gone to South Africa for work, remain critical to some of the neighboring countries, especially Lesotho and Mozambique. The 140,000 workers from Lesotho constitute about half of that country's male labor force and their remittances approximately half of its GNP. In October 1986, following an ANC land mine attack in the Eastern Transvaal, the South African government demonstrated its leverage over Mozambique's desperate economy by threatening to repatriate the estimated 170,000 illegal migrant workers and not permitting the 96,000 Mozambicans then employed to renew their contracts. These retaliatory measures were later modified, but the point had been made that Pretoria had it within its power to choke off Mozambique's single most important source of foreign exchange.

It is certainly true that the economic links between South Africa and its neighbors also benefit South Africa. Indeed, South Africa's total trade surplus with the Front Line States contributes materially to its overall positive balance of trade. But, given the perilous economic position of the Front Line States, the relationship is much more crucial to them than it is to South Africa—a fact South Africa has been able to demonstrate by periodic "technical" disruptions of the normal flow of goods and traffic. For all their political rhetoric, none of South Africa's neighbors have been in a position to adopt economic sanctions. Some of those direct neighbors could profit as conduits for South African trade and business activity if comprehensive sanctions were enacted. Even if the world community were prepared to assume the heavy financial burden of reducing the reliance of the Front Line States on South Africa—and the odds in the U.S. Congress are not good—such an effort would, at best, take many years to accomplish.

The inescapable fact remains: South Africa is the hub of the region and thus can hold its neighbors hostage. For all practical purposes this means that sanctions against South Africa are sanctions against southern Africa. Efforts to make the Front Line States more self-reliant, however desirable for economic as well as political reasons, are no substitute for political settlements between South Africa and its neighbors. Yet these will ultimately depend on progress toward a settlement within South Africa itself. No one has a greater stake in advancing this delicately interwoven process than the Front Line States themselves.

How Sanctions Really Work

The critical policy question is not how much pain economic sanctions can inflict on South Africa, but whether they contribute to peaceful change. Indeed, in most circumstances, the suggestion that policies designed to shrink the economic pie will facilitate the peaceful resolution of sociopolitical conflict would be dismissed as mad. Given the daunting growth requirements of the South African economy, the only conceivable justification for inflicting economic damage is the effect of sanctions in changing political behavior for the better. Moreover, that effect should take place reasonably quickly—before the long-term economic future of the country is permanently impaired. By these standards, the experience since the U.S. Congress overrode President Reagan's veto of the Comprehensive Anti-Apartheid Act in October 1986 is utterly negative.

This is not to imply that the U.S. sanctions, followed by somewhat milder measures by the European Community, explain everything that later happened on the South African political scene. But it is impossible to discern any of the positive effects sanctions advocates predicted. After all, except for those who may have pursued a hidden revolutionary agenda that "worse is better," the "message" of sanctions was supposed to make things better, not worse.

Instead, after the imposition of sanctions the South African government became more repressive, not less. The 1986 State of Emergency was extended and strengthened, the powers of the judiciary curtailed. On February 25, 1988, the political activities of 17 leading anti-apartheid organizations, including the United Democratic Front (UDF) and the Council of South African Trade Unions (COSATU), were banned. The list of banned persons, which had been dramatically reduced to single figures by 1986, once again grew with 18 restriction orders in March 1988 (meaning that the affected persons cannot be quoted or address public gatherings and are restricted in their movements). Talk of releasing Nelson Mandela and other long-term political prisoners ended, and the 1987 release of Govan Mbeki came to be officially described as a testing of the waters that failed.

The process of political reform has slowed as it approaches the limits beyond which the Botha government is not prepared to go: a system in which race classification remains the prime determinant of where people can live, which public schools they can attend, and, above all, who they can vote for.

The Group Areas Act which an original and unpublished report of the President's Council asked to be repealed, remains on the books, though local authorities have been granted discretion to allow "gray areas." In April, as if to reassure his moderate supporters that the National Party has not abandoned the cause of orderly reform, State President Botha signaled that he is prepared to draw blacks into the political system, but on his terms. He proposed the inclusion of blacks in a reconstituted, advisory President's Council that could be used both as a forum for constitutional negotiation and for political consultation before a new constitution is in place. He even suggested the possiblity of giving blacks a voice in the election of the state president, though the details were not spelled out. But in view of the continued insistence on a race-based system, the imprisonment of key black leaders like Nelson Mandela, and the banning of political activities of most black political organizations, the offer has found no takers from representative black leaders. As a result, the official political dialogue on power sharing at the national level remains in a state of suspended animation.

At the regional and local level, the government has conceded multiracial councils in which separately elected white and black officials can work together on matters of common concern. But the proposals for a black-led, multiracial provincial government for Natal and KwaZulu, worked out in long negotiations among representatives of all population groups, were effectively blocked by the government on the grounds that the envisaged nonracial lower chamber departed from the principle of a race-based system. Under National Party dogma, this constitutes a threat to minority rights.

The bottom line is that the white minority will not allow political control to pass into the hands of the black majority.

Indeed, after forty years in power, the National Party appears to be in no mood to cede control to any political rival, even if it means that the veneer of constitutional government wears steadily thinner in the process. As National Party ministers occasionally remind foreigners, "this is Africa."

The only area where reform continues is the economy, where the government is pursuing a policy of black economic "upliftment" and is making major investments in black housing, education, job creation and business opportunities. The infrastructure of long neglected townships like Alexandra is being improved, in part with the help of the army. As announced by Botha in opening Parliament on February 5, 1988, a radical turn of National Party economic policy toward privatization of the bloated public sector is supposed to release the funds to make the program possible. Plainly, the government hopes that, in tandem with an effective crushing of "radical" township activism, more and more blacks will come to realize the advantages of cooperation over the futility of violent confrontation with the vastly superior might of the state. While core political issues can not be suppressed for long, it would be unwise to dismiss this cooptation strategy out of hand. Some will be coopted. But in the end the government may discover that its approach further accentuates the contradictions between the economic and political status of South African blacks and intensifies the demand for full political participation.

One of the arguments in favor of sanctions—voiced most insistently by former Australian prime minister Malcolm Fraser—was that sanctions would finally force the trade-minded business establishment to use its full influence on the government. Yet the argument assumed a degree of political clout and government dependence on the business community that never existed. Most business leaders were critical of the government because apartheid collided with the requirements of an expanding industrial economy, and they were able to persuade the government of the need for significant socioeconomic reforms. But on the core political issues, their efforts to sway the government were, in the vivid phrase of Tony Bloom, the chairman of the Premier Group, like "throwing ping pong balls at a brick wall." Botha's blunt message was to stick to business and leave the politics to him.

Since the imposition of sanctions, moreover, what was an adversary relationship between government and business has become much more cooperative for the simple reason that there now is a common interest in beating sanctions. Inevitably, the dependence of business on government has increased. (A telling illustration: the Federated Chamber of Industries, which before sanctions pushed for political reform, replaced the executives who were identified with this liberal approach and has adopted a much lower political profile. As for Tony Bloom, he has decided to leave South Africa and move to Britain.)

This convergence of interests seems likely to persist since South Africa's recent economic performance, while suprisingly good, is vulnerable. While U.S.-South African trade was down 44 percent over the first nine months of 1987, the volume of exports was up, largely because the low exchange rate of the rand made South African goods highly competitive in new markets, especially in Asia.[5] European tourism staged a strong comeback. As previously in Rhodesia, import substitution contributed to domestic growth. However, as renewed domestic demand sucked in imports, the trade surplus shrank, forcing an increase in interest rates. Inflation in 1988 remained in double digits (14.5 percent). With foreign lending no longer available to finance a trade deficit, and effectively barred from access to the international financial institutions, South Africa's economy is performing without a safety net—a heavy burden for a country with massive development needs.

White politics in South Africa since the imposition of sanctions has been characterized by a powerful surge of right-wing Afrikaner opposition to the government, the rallying of English-speaking voters to the National Party, and the fragmentation of the white liberal opposition. Indeed, Botha's decision to call an early election for the white chamber of parliament for May 6, 1987, reflected the judgment that sanctions would provide him with a rallying cry to unite white voters behind his government in a show of defiance to foreign pressure. Appealing to white anxieties over security, the National Party increased its commanding majority in the 178-seat chamber from 127 to 133 seats, mainly because the English-speaking vote flocked to it as the party of orderly reform.

On the other hand, close to half the Afrikaans-speaking voters, who make up about 60 percent of the white electorate, deserted to the far-right Conservatives. This shocked the National Party, which has always seen itself as the legitimate political voice of Afrikanerdom. It is now haunted by the trauma of another Afrikaner leader, Jan Smuts, whose United Party lost power in 1948 because his English-speaking support could not make up for the loss of Afrikaner backing. The worst losers of the elections were the Progressives, whose representation in parliament dropped from 27 to 20. With 23 seats—including 5 gains in the Transvaal platteland—the Conservatives thus took over as the official opposition party.

The creditable performance of two reform-minded defectors from the National Party seemed to provide a ray of hope that a new Independent Movement, led by Afrikaners, might gain momentum. Wynand Malan, who quit the Nationalists in parliament to run as an independent, handily retained his seat, while Dennis Worrall, formerly South Africa's ambassador to Britain, came within 39 votes of a spectacular upset of one of the prime contenders for Botha's succession, Minister for Constitutional Affairs Chris Heunis. (Replying to suggestions by some American commentators that his defection from the government was one of the positive results of sanctions, Worrall sighed later that if it had not been for sanctions, he could easily have won those 39 votes.) However, Malan and Worrall fell out over direction of the new movement, leaving the liberal white opposition in disarray, with little chance of attracting additional support from the ranks of the National Party.

The sanctions issue will in the near term be played out in the shadow of a right wing surge in white South African politics. On one hand, one of South Africa's leading political analysis, Professor Lawrence Schlemmer of the University of the Witwatersrand, estimates that for the National Party to lose its present parliamentary majority would require a 15 percent swing towards the Conservatives—something he does not regard as likely nationwide. While in two Transvaal by-elections in March 1988, Conservative candidates were able to treble their majorities, the swing there was only 2.5 percent. On the other hand, he projects that if an election is held in 1989, the Conservatives could increase their present strength from 23 to 62 seats. This would still leave them 22 seats short of a parliamentary majority. But such an advance would send shock waves through a National Party that has come to see a huge absolute majority as the natural order of things. Moreover, the outcome of municipal elections in October 1988, could greatly strengthen the Conservative Party's organizational base for the next round of general elections (to all three chambers) that, under the present constitution, will have to be held by early 1990 at the latest. Further Conservative Party inroads in the Transvaal and Free State, once the impregnable Afrikaner bastions of the National Party strength, are likely to be particularly traumatic to the government.

The salient point, missed by many anti-apartheid campaigners abroad, is that the National Party now sees the rise of the right wing as a far more serious threat to its political survival than either international sanctions or internal black revolt. To be seen to be knuckling under to outside pressures in these circumstances would only add to this threat.

Botha's attempt to play for time by putting off the elections until 1992 has been frustrated by the refusal of the leader of the coloured Labor Party, the Reverend Allan Hendrickse, to support the necessary constitutional amendment unless the government commits itself to the repeal of the Group Areas Act. Outraged over Hendrickse's obstinacy, Botha fired him from the cabinet, but thus far Hendrickse has stood his ground.

The very reforms that most blacks and much of the world dismissed as inadequate were seen by many whites as the thin end of the wedge. The reforms departed from orthodox apartheid: ending the white monopoly in parliament by creating chambers for coloureds and Asians, recognizing black rights to permanent residence in so-called "white urban areas" and restoring black citizenship, repealing of the pass laws and influx control, breaking down of "petty apartheid" in public facilities, repealing of the Immorality and Mixed Marriages Acts, and permitting the de facto emergence of integrated "gray areas" in major cities. In the economic sphere, poorer whites felt threatened by the abolition of job reservation, the emergence of a powerful, recognized black trade union movement, the integration of the work place, the narrowing of wage gaps, and, not the least, the shifting of public resources toward "black upliftment." The deepest recession since the 1930s fed all these anxieties among poorer whites.

For the right, the government's internationally condemned response to the outbreak of unrest in 1984 was not tough enough. So, too, the prohibition of political activities by 17 anti-apartheid groups in February 1988 was "too little, too late." Judging by the by-election results a few days later, the February crackdown certainly failed to impress the voters. Botha was also hurt by the right's belief that in pursuing reformist policies, he was responding to foreign—and particularly American—pressure. (Exaggerated notions of foreign influence are a common denominator between white right wingers and black militants in South Africa.)

No politician in any country likes to be seen as surrendering to foreign pressure, least of all Afrikaner politicians. From the days of the Dutch East India Company to the Great Trek and the Boer war, there has been a powerful isolationist streak in the Afrikaner volk; they have seen themselves as a beleaguered minority battling a hostile environment. Those in the West who campaign for the isolation of South Africa effectively reinforce this psyche. No one even fleetingly familiar with three centuries of South African history could conclude that Afrikaners are not prepared to make economic sacrifices to defend their identity against outsiders. History aside, the proposition that any people will commit what they perceive as political suicide rather than endure a measure of economic pain strains credulity. It is no victory for peaceful change when well-educated professionals unhappy about their government's drift into greater repression and worried about the future of their children decide to leave, and those who do not have these qualms—or the option to leave—stay behind. If sanctions were to threaten the living standards of whites, the poorer whites first affected will hardly urge their government to abandon apartheid to get the sanctions lifted but will rather support the far right instead. If sanctions provoke economic downturns, they will revive fears among poor whites of black economic competition and so play into the hands of the far right.

But what about the impact of sanctions on the country's black majority? Has the willingness to suffer asserted by leading black advocates of sanctions any reasonable prospect of translating into political gain?

There is little doubt that many—though by no means all—South African blacks welcomed the Congressional override of President Reagan's veto of the Comprehensive Anti-Apartheid Act as a tangible expression of support in the struggle against a repressive government. But South African blacks expect more than sympathy from the West—and especially from the Western superpower. At the end of the day, only results matter.

In the heady days of 1984–86, when many South African blacks—and television viewers abroad—deluded themselves that the black struggle had reached the stage where a final push from abroad might make the apartheid system collapse or plead for terms, sanctions seemed to hold out that promise. But that euphoria has been replaced with a somber realization that the South African government remains by all odds the most powerful party in the conflict and that its overthrow is not anywhere near the horizon.

When sanctions had negative effects, their most prominent advocates were soon criticizing the American and European sanctions as half-hearted. In a BBC interview the Reverend Allan Boesak conceded that limited sanctions and disinvestment were threatening to give South African blacks the worst of all worlds: a weakened economy, less responsive employers, and more rather than less, political repression. In a line since echoed by Archbishop Desmond Tutu and the leadership of COSATU, Boesak appealed for economic and political boycotts so total and drastic as to force the Botha government to its knees quickly, before lasting damage is done to the country's economic prospects.

The yearning for a quick and relatively painless scenario for black liberation is understandable enough. But the unpalatable truth is that it represents wishful thinking on a dangerous scale. A coercive strategy to defeat the South African government would in the final analysis have to rely on a direct and major military intervention by the major powers. It is revealing, perhaps, that so far this option has been broached only by Ireland's Connor Cruise O'Brien, a man with an admirable trait of thinking the unthinkable.[6] But thus far his startling suggestion has not found favor with even the most militant anti-apartheid activists. And as Britain found out in the Boer War, military intervention in South Africa is not a decision to be taken lightly.

Clearly, the appeal of sanctions is precisely that it is a soft, relatively cost-free option. Protectionist measures like the ban on South African coal, which has led to the layoff of 10,000 black miners, are particularly attractive politically, since they can be given moral gloss as a "blow against apartheid"—a true "two-fer," as Senator Paul Simon of the coal-mining state of Illinois and chairman of the Senate Subcommittee on Africa acknowledged with disarming candor during the debate of the 1986 Comprehensive Anti-Apartheid Act.

It is a sad irony that the impulse to "do something" about one of the great moral and political dramas of our age, which spawned the sanctions drive, has sharply reduced the West's ability to influence the course of events. President Botha decided, sometime in the spring of 1986, that the price for inducing the U.S. Congress not to vote for sanctions was too high. Since then, P.W. Botha seemed to act like a man liberated of the need to cope with meddlesome foreigners, especially Americans. High level dialogue between the U.S. and the South African governments on internal reform issues has essentially ceased and given way to evermore acrimonious recitations of grievances—both in public and in private.

Before then, Botha's cabinet used to at least consider what was known as "the American factor." The hope for improved relations with Washington and the realization that it had to pay some price for enabling the Reagan Administration to resist the pressure for sanctions became significant elements in government decision making. On a number of occasions, this factor helped to tip the scales, encouraging moves toward reform, albeit limited and incremental, and, sometimes but by no means always, inhibiting internal and regional misconduct. The limit of U.S. influence depended on P.W. Botha's assessment of his government's internal and regional security requirements and his judgment of what the traffic of white South African politics could bear.

Especially after the outbreak of township unrest in 1984—ironically touched off by the "reform" that allowed coloured and Indians into the previously "whites only" political system—these judgments provoked more and more international condemnation. Botha's name became synonymous with ruthless repression. But in his own perception, if not in the eyes of most black South Africans and the outside world, Botha was a politically courageous reformer who was doing more to change the country than all his predecessors combined, even at the risk of splitting his core constituency. Yet his South African version of glasnost seemed to make the West more, not less, hostile.

With increasing bitterness, he discovered that none of his concessions satisfied his international critics, let alone restored a degree of normalcy to his government's relations with the West. In 1984, he briefly entertained hopes of breaking out of his status as an international pariah. He traveled to Europe, and despite embarrassing attempts to keep him at arm's length, the event was billed as a success in South Africa. But it grated on him that while his rival adversaries, Archbishop Desmond Tutu and Chief Mangosothu Buthelezi, were each received by President Reagan, such a meeting with him was obviously regarded as too great a political liability, as indeed it would have been.

When significant reforms like the repeal of the pass laws were dismissed in the U.S. Congress as cosmetic, Botha reached the conclusion that only the complete transfer of power to the black majority would satisfy his American Congressional critics. Plainly, to his thinking if it took political suicide to stave off sanctions, they were the lesser evil. Similarly, the threat of

Commonwealth sanctions did not deter Botha from authorizing the May 18, 1986, cross-border raids on purported ANC targets in Botswana, Zimbabwe, and Zambia, even though he must have realized that the raids would effectively destroy the negotiating initiative of the Commonwealth Eminent Persons Group and provoke them into issuing a highly negative report. As he kept telling visitors, it was preferable to "call the bluff" rather than be "held up for ransom." No escalation of sanctions would change that simple calculus. In short, the more Western demands escalated ("moving the goalposts" was the South African phrase), the less adequate Western leverage became to achieve them. As he had threatened in his disastrous "Rubicon speech" to the 1985 National Party congress in Durban, "don't push us too far."

The congressional override of President Reagan's veto of the Comprehensive Anti-Apartheid Act on October 2, 1986, confirmed Botha's view that the executive branch had lost control over American policy toward South Africa to a Congress that was dealing with the issue primarily in terms of domestic political expedience. That his own behavior contributed to this result was something Botha refused to acknowledge—after all, his first order of priorities was to solve his own political problems rather than those of the American president.

The imposition of sanctions and the sharp deterioration in bilateral relations between Washington and Pretoria has also had an adverse effect on the ability of the United States to conduct effective regional diplomacy. It is hard to imagine that the U.S. could have brokered the Nkomati Accord between South Africa and Mozambique and the Lusaka disengagement agreement between South Africa and Angola if the Comprehensive Anti-Apartheid Act had been in effect in 1984. The ever more truculent South African attitude toward the United States, and in particular Botha's visceral resentments, have hampered American efforts to restrain South African cross-border strikes and to encourage compliance with the Nkomati Accord.

The most critical test, however, is whether the United States can still broker an Angolan-Namibian agreement, matching the withdrawal of 40,000 Cuban troops from Angola with the

withdrawal of South African forces and the implementation of
Security Council Resolution 435 on Namibian independence.
Following another in a series of visits to Luanda by Assistant
Secretary of State for African Affairs Chester A. Crocker in
January 1988, the State Department announced that both
Angola and Cuba, the latter represented for the first time, have
accepted the principle of complete Cuban withdrawal, without
an indefinite Cuban residual force. At the same time, there were
indications that the Soviet government was getting weary of the
seemingly open-ended conflict involving massive shipments of
arms to the MPLA government, running at a rate of over $1
billion a year in 1987 (compared to U.S. assistance to UNITA of
$15 million a year) when these shipments evidently failed to
force a decisive military victory for the Angolan government.

The Botha government, and especially the South African
military, have been watching the American negotiating effort
with growing disdain. Defense Minister Magnus Malan typified
this attitude when he went on South African television in
March, 1988, with a plump bid to settle the matter directly with
Moscow, without the benefit of American mediation. The
Soviets, he said pointedly "have clearly taken note of the
weakening influence of the United States in southern Africa".
The overture, which followed a secret meeting between Malan
and the Soviet ambassador in Lesotho, was contemptu-
ously dismissed by Moscow. The dispatch of a fresh Cuban
armed force of some 5,000 men into southern Angola in March
seemed designed to signal to the South Africans that their
continued involvement in Angola would carry increasing costs
in men and equipment. In early May, Angolan, Cuban, South
African, and American negotiators met in London, but a
skeptical Botha warned against over-optimism. His negotiators
were expected to play a delaying game. Synchronising an
acceptable timetable for Cuban withdrawal with the cessation of
outside assistance to Jonas Savimbi's UNITA movement and
South African implementation of Resolution 435 is an intricate
exercise under the best of circumstances and thus lends itself to
such tactics. The military, fiscal and political costs that South
Africa would have to pay for continuing the indefinite and

inconclusive conflict are at least as great as they are for the other parties. Nevertheless, neither the South African government's preoccupation with its right-wing opposition at home, nor its growing anti-Americanism allows for much hope that Crocker's dogged mediating effort will produce success before the end of the Reagan Administration.

What the South African government seemed to be signaling was that it will not permit the United States and other Western countries to replace a policy of "constructive engagement" with a policy of "selective engagement"—that is, it will not allow the West to impose punitive economic measures while carrying on as before in other areas; for instance, in regional diplomacy.

That same South African attitude seems to apply to private and public Western funding of organizations and activities designed to challenge the apartheid system and build black leadership and bargaining power. On August 13, 1987, State President Botha served notice that he intended to shut off foreign funding of activities designed for "undermining the state and promoting extra-parliamentary politics." In March 1988 his government followed through by proposing the "Promotion of Orderly Internal Politics Bill," which bars any person or organization from receiving "any money which is intended to be used, or in the discretion of that organization or person may be used to further, propagate, pursue or oppose any political aim or object." Depending on how the minister of justice chooses to define political activity, this law could deal a serious blow to Western private and official efforts to reach out to the victims of apartheid and maintain lines of communication.

The amounts involved are substantial. According to Western diplomatic estimates, the total of private and official assistance from abroad received by anti-apartheid and human rights groups in 1987 came to at least $250 million. For many anti-apartheid groups foreign funds have represented most of their budget. Particularly seriously affected are the Congress of South African Trade Unions (COSATU), which has been funded heavily by foreign trade unions, and the various activities funded through the South African Council of Churches with contributions from the World Council of Churches and other international church organizations. Another obvious target is the Institute for Democratic Alternatives (IDASA), founded by former Progressive Federal Party leaders Frederick Van Zyl Slabbert and Alex Boraine, which organized the much publicized meeting between some 60 prominent whites, mostly Afrikaners, and representatives of the ANC in Dakar in 1987. Botha has taken the position that such private diplomacy undercuts the position of his government.

American official assistance in the fields of education, entrepreneurial and trade union training, nutrition, legal assistance, and community self-help projects has been funded at a level of about $25 million a year. Virtually all other Western embassies in South Africa have been running similar programs. A heavy-handed South African effort to interfere with them would probably only lead to decisions to divert these funds to activities outside South Africa over which Pretoria has no jurisdiction. Nevertheless, Western governments would be deprived of a valuable tool to maintain contacts within the black community in South Africa and to offer it encouragement and practical help in developing leadership and organizational cohesion.

The United States also lost influence through the mass exodus of multinational companies. The 80-odd American companies that decided to sell their assets cheaply to South African interests left under no illusion that their departure made a contribution to the fight against apartheid. They left out of weariness: for most of them their South African business accounted for less than 1 percent of their global turnover, and the cost of tangling with the disinvestment movement in the United States had simply become disproportionately high. State and municipal governments in the U.S. began barring companies doing business in South Africa from bidding for public contracts, and in December 1987 Congressman Charles Rangel slipped an amendment into the mammoth Budget Reconciliation Act that ended credits granted to American companies for taxes paid to the South African government, thus exposing them to crushing double taxation of 72 percent.

The net effect of these departures has been to replace American employers who were under the discipline of the

Sullivan Code of fair employment practices with other employers who are not. Over the ten years since the code was
introduced, the signatory companies spent $280 million for black
advancement and followed enlightened employment practices
that set standards for other employers as well. Yet now only
about half of the signatories are still in South Africa.

Given this melancholy record of waning Western relevance
and growing South African obstinacy, what realistic options are
left for the members of the alliance? Collective handwringing
will hardly make up for reduced influence, though it will no
doubt be featured at countless international conferences and
more or less scholarly symposiums. The brash challenge by
South Africa's representative to the United Nations to the
Security Council in March 1988 to "do your damnedest" is one
that many will want to take up. (Foreign Minister "Pik" Botha
proudly took personal credit for this sample of Boer braggado-
cio.)

As a matter of political realism, it will be difficult, if not
impossible, for the U.S. and other Western countries to back out
of the cul-de-sac of economic sanctions. Even if it were possible
in terms of domestic politics, lifting the sanctions now on the
books would inevitably be seen as rewarding South African
government behavior that in several respects has become even
worse than it was at the time the original sanctions were
imposed. At the minimum, lifting sanctions would have to be
tied to the South African government's adherence to its own
international undertakings, such as implementation of Resolution 435 in return for an agreement on full Cuban troop
withdrawal, and strict observance of the Nkomati Accord.
Whatever conditions the alliance might set for lifting some or all
of the sanctions would have to address the political problem for
the South African government of seeming to surrender to
outside pressures. But the quiet diplomacy that this would
require is precluded by the public attention the issue has
attracted and, in the U.S., the involvement of Congress.
Unfortunately, it is much easier politically to impose sanctions
than to find face-saving ways of lifting them.

Still, while reversing the current sanctions may not be feasible, there is no reason that the West must travel further down a dead-end street. Just because right-wing diehards in South Africa and left-wing activists converge in their dreams of an isolated South Africa—and the South African government is daring the world to do it—is simply not a good enough reason for Western governments to indulge them.

Even though its influence has diminished, the West must remain engaged. The present circumstances do not lend themselves to revived mediation efforts along the lines of the 1986 Commonwealth initiative, but there will come a time when the major players in the South African drama realize that the costs of continued conflict exceed those of compromise, and mediation will become possible. It is hard to see such a turning point coming until the domineering figure of P.W. Botha has left the scene, but the moment will surely come. For the members of the alliance to be able to perform this facilitating function requires keeping open the lines of communication to all the necessary parties—from the African National Congress, Inkatha, and the UDF, to the full spectrum of white, Indian, and coloured opinion. While communicating with the ANC as one of the key parties is essential, recognizing it as the "sole legitimate representative of the South African people" and as a South African government-in-exile would be a major blunder since it would cripple the ability of Western countries to play a role in bringing all the parties together.

There may well be useful divisions of labor: under present circumstances, for example, the Thatcher government may have better access to the Botha government than any other Western government. What will matter is that the message passed be the same. The principles outlined by George Shultz provide a good start. Involving the presidents of the Front Line States will be crucial, given their vital interest in a settlement and their relationship with the black liberation movements. The 1986 Eminent Persons Group initiative, though foiled by South Africa's actions, nevertheless demonstrated the positive potential of the Commonwealth.

Keeping the lines of communication open also remains important in the context of Southern African regional relations—in spite of the reduced American influence with Pretoria and the South African government's current predilection for a mailed-fist approach in its neighborly relations. (As Africans know, cornered elephants usually turn vicious.) A break in communications with Pretoria would dash any hope, however remote, of it agreeing to the implementation of Security Council Resolution 435 for the independence of Namibia. The idea that the imposition of mandatory sanctions will effectively compel South Africa to withdraw from the territory is political fantasy, especially so when sanctions are already being threatened—and imposed—for internal behavior.

In the meantime, the alliance should coordinate its efforts to strengthen the Front Line States and reduce their vulnerability to South African pressure. Rehabilitating and expanding the port of Beira and the Beira rail corridor is an obvious example. The alliance should also be responsive to the requests from the Front Line States to upgrade their border security. While they cannot match the military might of their neighbor, they may be able to raise the costs to South Africa of recurrent cross-border raids. The South African government is highly sensitive about casualties among (white) national servicemen, which it can ill conceal, and the loss of sophisticated equipment, like helicopters.

Within South Africa itself, the Western allies should cooperate in efforts to help the disadvantaged majority develop the skills and the leadership it will need to play its rightful role in a post-apartheid South Africa. While the new restrictions on foreign funding may constrain some of these efforts, Pretoria may still permit such important educational programs as scholarships for black students for study both abroad and at South African universities. Similarly, programs to advance black entrepreneurship and executive skills not only strengthen black bargaining power but also the odds for the survival of the free enterprise system, which is so vital to the economic future of post-apartheid South Africa.

So, too, maintaining links with South African universities—and not just the racially integrated English-speaking universities but also the Afrikaans universities—is absolutely essential. The idea of an academic boycott is an affront to Western principles of the free exchange of ideas. In the same spirit, it is important that official grants for visits to the West be given not just to the victims of apartheid but also to white opinion-makers. In many cases, exposure to the bracing environment of an open Western society has been a milestone event in the lives of even conservatively inclined white South Africans. Finally, it is important for the West to facilitate communication among South Africans themselves, both in South Africa and abroad.

These are modest proposals, geared to the reduced circumstances of Western influence. No doubt they will find no favor with those who still delude themselves and others that the West could "end apartheid now," if only it mustered the will. So long as these people continue to believe that the West is the determining factor in the South African drama, they will be disappointed by any policy the United States and its allies adopt. But as they notice that their activist prescriptions to isolate South Africa are producing perverse results contrary to those desired, perhaps they will finally realize that there is no quick fix.

In particular, the new president of the United States will bear a heavy responsibility for rescuing the South African issue from degenerating into a convenient political football; a mere extension of our domestic politics. Such a degeneration would be destructive not only to American influence in South Africa but to relations with allies as well. It would undermine any effective American leadership. The next president must therefore take the lead in rebuilding a national consensus on the issue. Since his views on South Africa will be seen in the broader context of his views on racial justice and equality, he will have to speak—and act—with a degree of conviction, commitment and sensitivity that leaves no doubt where he stands on this fundamental issue. Only once all doubts have been removed on this point will it be possible to carry on a debate on South Africa as it should be conducted—a reasoned debate about means in a nation that agrees about the ends. Early in his administration the president must take the initiative to restore a degree of trust and cooperation between Congress and the executive branch without which no foreign policy can be sustained.

But the congressional leadership also bears a heavy responsibility and must meet the president halfway. Congress has the constitutional responsibilities to advise and consent, but, in every sense of the word, it is constitutionally incapable of leadership in foreign policy. The erosion of presidential leadership in the field of foreign affairs cannot be allowed to continue. So long as it does, the prospect for any steadfast, sustainable, and serious U.S. policy toward South Africa—one the alliance can support—remains bleak.

Notes

1. Leadership, December 1, 1987.
2. In a chapter of a forthcoming book by R. W. Bethlehem entitled, *Sanctions and the Processes of Adjustment.*
3. *Commentary* July 1987, (Vol. 84, No. 1). Professor Peter Berger and Bobby Godsell have argued that, far from it being "too late" for negotiations, it may well be too early.
4. G.G. Maasdorp, "Economic and Political Implications of Regional Cooperation in Southern Africa," *South African Journal of Economics*, Johannesburg, Vol. 54, No. 2, pp. 151-171.
5. *Financial Times*, March 15, 1988.
6. *Atlantic*, "What Can Become of South Africa," March, 1986.

South Africa and the Western Alliance

Donald F. McHenry

South Africa, East-West relations, and the Middle East conflict would appear in almost any list of the five or ten most important international tensions. South Africa, however, is distinctly different from most of the others on the list. The difference is that neither of the superpowers nor their closest allies is directly involved in South Africa or, for that matter, places a high priority on the southern African region. In addition, although the situation in South Africa is one of extraordinary cruelty, it is unlikely to have an incendiary effect on international peace and security. Rather, apartheid has a slow corrosive effect on East-West relations and on relations between the people of southern Africa, particularly South Africa, and the countries of the Western alliance. The corrosion results from the indirect involvement of external powers, the emerging perception that the West and the East have taken sides on the ultimate outcome, and, so long as it is not resolved, the intrusive effect of apartheid on seemingly unrelated issues in the United Nations and other international organizations.

Assumptions of the Allies

Can apartheid, or more specifically, differences in approaches among the countries of the Western alliance adversely affect Western unity? If so, what can Western countries do to minimize the effect? Even if the effect on the Western alliance is small, are there cooperative measures the alliance might take to promote the end of apartheid and reduce the perception in Africa and among many developing countries that the West tacitly or indirectly supports the South African government?

In the analysis that follows, I make little effort to explore in detail developments in South and southern Africa. Rather my

120

view of the direction of events is implicit, and the analysis is
limited to examining issues in the area to the extent that they
involve debate and decision within the Western alliance. Any
effort to analyze the effect of apartheid on the Western alliance
requires recognizing a number of assumptions that are often
overlooked or simply given lip service:

- There is unlikely to be a quick fix for the situation in South
  Africa. The South African government is unlikely to demonstrate the vision or take the decisive action that would
  amount to a breakthrough toward a solution. Nor is the
  black majority currently either internally or externally
  capable of mounting the kind of pressure that would cause
  the South African government to change its course. Rather,
  Pretoria is likely to continue its current approach of limited
  and insufficient—though significant—concessions while it
  searches for a more acceptable way of maintaining white
  domination. The likelihood, therefore, is for a long struggle,
  increasingly violent, increasingly polarized, with the basis of
  accommodation increasingly narrowed. Further, despite the
  reservoir of goodwill that, amazingly, remains among blacks,
  there are increasing signs that some among them and die-
  hard whites may be unable to undertake the programs of
  accommodation and reconstruction that will face a new
  South Africa. In short, those who have counseled slow
  change in the interest of stability may have made instability
  unavoidable.
- Arguments that the West agrees that apartheid must end but
  differs with Africans on the means will fall on increasingly
  deaf ears. Differences over means are not necessarily mere
  cover for support of an immoral status quo, but the failure to
  support a means at least as effective as that one opposes
  does call into question support of the end itself.
- South Africans themselves will have to find the solution to
  their own problems. However, as in the case of Jews in
  Germany, it may be fairly asked in the future what the West
  did to assist in an hour of need.

- Analyses that see the issues through an East-West prism are not currently valid but will become increasingly so as the West is identified with the South African government and is accused of placing its economic and political priorities over human dignity. In the meantime, an increasingly sophisticated East, though never willing to make South Africa a priority, will do just enough to gain credit for assistance against South Africa. Young South African blacks will become anti-capitalist and anti-Western. In other words, those, including South Africans, who are concerned about the advance of communist influence in South Africa may be following a strategy that insures the outcome they fear most.

Respected research by such groups as the Thomas Commission in *Time Running Out* and the Advisory Group to the Secretary of State have eliminated as a red herring arguments that the United States and the West would be unacceptably hurt if there were an interruption in access to minerals from South Africa. So do the authors of this volume. South Africa cannot afford to withhold minerals from the market, nor for that matter, could a successor government, whatever its racial composition or political disposition. Stockpiles, alternative sources, and alternative materials are or could be available. Neither is the old canard about the Cape route now taken seriously by American military strategists, if it ever was.

The United States and Europe: Different Approaches

Neither the United States nor Europe is monolithic in their approaches to South Africa and the region of southern Africa. In Europe, Britain, and to a somewhat lesser extent, the Federal Republic are to the right, with France and southern Europe in the middle while the Netherlands, Denmark, Norway, and the other Scandinavians are to the left. Thousands of European immigrants entered South Africa as permanent residents during the 1960s and 1970s. If American experience is any guide, not only do those new arrivals constitute a drag on the policies of their former countries, but they also join the most conservative elements of South African society. For example, the German right has been a strong supporter for an internal settlement in Namibia. On the other hand, perhaps because of embarrassment, the Dutch background of the Afrikaner has not been a major impediment to a Dutch policy strongly critical of South Africa.

Europe is also closer to South Africa economically. It is a principal consumer of South African raw materials and a marketer of such important South African exports as gold and diamonds. South Africa is a principal consumer of European manufactured goods. More specifically, Britain, West Germany, and France rank with the United States and Japan among the top five trading partners of South Africa and currently are more loathe than the United States to risk that relationship by imposing sanctions. To their credit, it should be noted that these countries have traditionally been reluctant, even in the face of provocation, to use economic measures to accomplish political objectives.

Europe's colonial past has receded but still colors African views of it. There is a pervasive feeling among Africans that much of Europe shares white South Africa's views of Africans.

A number of other factors also account for a difference between Europe and American approaches to South Africa. The governments of Europe are central rather than federal; significantly, by 1987, 23 American states and 175 cities had acted on their own to institute sanctions against South Africa. Moreover, the European states are parliamentary, so there is no separation between the executive branch and the legislature. It is thus less likely that public pressure on more vulnerable legislators can influence the policy of the executive. European countries, more homogeneous than the United States, have less of a tradition of responsiveness to pressure groups on foreign policy issues, even if the difference is overstated: farmers and other economic groups do have demonstrable influence, and Europeans, while quick to criticize the United States for responding to internal politics over South Africa, have no hesitation in responding to their own internal politics. European corporate structures are traditionally less responsive to shareholder pressure—and do not expect pressure on social issues—than are their American counterparts. Finally, European governments seem more relaxed about the existence of offensive practices in other countries, not that they approve but that they accept reality in the almost cynical belief that life goes on.

None of this is to suggest that Europe is immune to pressure from its publics on the South Africa issue. Shell Oil has been the object of a boycott and some retail establishments—the Dutch firm, Makro, for instance—have reported increasing sales losses because they carry South African goods or have outlets in South Africa. In addition, major British banks have left South Africa after vowing that they would not do so, in part because their South African business was sluggish and not worth the risk of increased capital but also because they wished to do business elsewhere in Africa.

On the American side there is no history of American-South African relations, and the pull of "kith and kin" is minimal to nonexistent. There is a racial factor: black American political power, on the rise, is a potent factor in close political races. Increasingly, on their own and in alliance with other groups, blacks have followed the well worn path of Irish, Polish, Greek, Italian, and Jewish Americans in exerting ethnic group influence on American foreign policy.

At the same time, it is a frequent European mistake to attribute the more critical American policy toward South Africa solely or even largely to the American racial situation. Rather, the specific concern is in line with more general American traditions. Even before the rise of the largely black lobbying group, TransAfrica, in the late 1970s, South Africa was already an issue of major concern to white church organizations and college students. The current American coalition favoring tougher action against South Africa brings together blacks, churches, youth, labor unions, civil libertarians, and others.

Moreover, historically, South Africa's own actions have been the major force behind each tightening of American policy. The repression of Soweto students, the murder of Steve Biko, and repression of youths in townships in the mid-1980s, followed by draconian emergency measures, led to the passage of tough

American legislation. South Africa's move to censor television, photographic, and written reports itself is an acknowledgment of the effects of its own actions. However much this cynicism is to be deplored, the analysis suggests that Americans operate on the principle of "out of sight out of mind."

The American position of world leadership, however, makes it all but impossible to avoid the apartheid issue. The disillusionment of recent years notwithstanding, much of the world looks uniquely to the United States to be the advocate of equal rights and justice. That perception, combined with the mistaken view that American power is such that apartheid could be brought to its knees if the United States so willed, puts the United States in a position quite apart from its European allies. And, indeed the United States has been in the lead on the apartheid issue. It was the United States that unilaterally declared an embargo on the sale of arms and military equipment to South Africa in 1963. And it was the United States that took the lead in making the arms embargo mandatory following the death of Biko.

This does not mean that there is unity in the United States over South Africa. The Reagan Administration and some well-placed conservatives argue for a closer relationship with South Africa on several grounds: because such a relationship would better position the United States to influence positive change; or because they see some common interest with South Africa in the East-West conflict or in access to strategic minerals. Finally, although they would never admit it, it is hard to escape the feeling that they have some sympathy with South African arguments.

Historically, the range of differences within official Washington has not been large no matter which political party has been in office. The differences that did exist seldom called into question basic policy. All of that changed, however, with the advent of the Reagan Administration and its policy of "constructive engagement" in 1981. By 1986 the American Congress repudiated the Reagan policy and in the Comprehensive Anti-Apartheid Act of 1986, passed over the Mr. Reagan's veto, mandated a tougher and more publicly critical policy toward South Africa.

Sanctions: A Diversionary Smokescreen

Much of the debate on South Africa revolves around sanctions: are they effective and appropriate to pressure South Africa to end apartheid? Sanctions as a weapon against South Africa have been advocated for almost three decades. Sanctions, it is argued, are the one peaceful means of influencing South Africa and avoiding large-scale bloodshed. The advocates of sanctions argue—though whether they believe is open to question—that South Africa could not continue its policies in the face of universally adopted sanctions. In this view, only the selfish economic interests of South Africa's "major trading partners" enables South Africa to prosper.

The argument against the use of sanctions is equally sweeping: Sanctions do not work. Sanctions hurt precisely the ones— black Africans—they are supposed to help. Economic growth will do more to end apartheid than sanctions.

There is, to be sure, a more principled argument against the use of sanctions, but it is frequently shrouded by expressions of concern over effectiveness or over effects on blacks and neighboring southern African countries. As noted above, Europeans, particularly the British, have in general opposed using sanctions for political pressure. However, even they have made notable departures from this position. For instance, they went to the United Nations for sanctions against Rhodesia when sanctions were the only alternative to force. They supported the American call in the UN Security Council for sanctions against Iran as a way of pressuring Iran to end the Iran-Iraq war. And they cut off all ties with Libya and Syria after concluding that both countries were involved in acts of terrorism. In the case of South Africa, despite withering criticism in the Commonwealth, the effect of sanctions against South Africa on the British economy, already having to adjust to changing economic conditions, is deemed unacceptable. Besides, the British argue, the list of candidates for sanctions and the number of requests for their imposition would be endless.

While Europeans have been relatively consistent on the question of sanctions, the United States has not. The same Americans who argue that sanctions do not work and should not be applied against South Africa show no reluctance, indeed are anxious, to apply sanctions against Iran, Nicaragua, Cuba, Poland, and the Soviet Union. Nor are they hesitant to pressure America's European allies to follow the American lead. It is clear, therefore, that the object of sanctions is as important as effectiveness.

Behind all the arguments there is a strong flavor of self-interest. In 1978, for example, during discussions among Western allies aimed at determining, on a contingency basis, which sanctions might be effective against South Africa it was difficult to agree. It quickly became apparent that conclusions were driven by the effect of sanctions on the imposing country, not on South Africa. Even in the instance of the Comprehensive Anti-Apartheid Act of 1986, it can be argued that the American Congress applied sanctions consistent with the trade protection-ist mood of the times. The legislation specifically granted exemptions for items of strategic importance to the United States while excluding coal and agricultural products that important political constituencies wished to exclude anyway.

In general, both sides of the sanctions argument are simplistic. South Africa has had considerable time to prepare for economic sanctions. South Africa is strong economically and it is resource-ful enough to exploit the schisms and greed that exist in the international community. South Africa is capable of meeting its own needs, though at additional cost and perhaps some sacrifice in quality. Finally, it is true that at the outset the imposition of sanctions or the threat of any outside force is likely to promote unified resistance among whites—the retreat into the laager, in South African vernacular.

But it is also a mistake to argue that sanctions have no effect. One year after the Comprehensive Anti-Apartheid Act of 1986, it was widely argued that sanctions had not worked, even that they had had the opposite of their intended effect on South Africa. In truth, only a fool could argue that the limited steps mandated by the American Congress would have decisively influenced South African policy. Not only were the sanctions limited in their application by the United States, there were no measures of similar scope taken by other countries with significant trade with South Africa. The Act anticipated the need for sanctions by other countries and so specifically directed the president to persuade other countries to follow the American lead.

However, the effort in the European Economic Community to take stronger action was blocked, largely by the British. In 1987, on the first anniversary of the Act, the General Accounting Office reported to Congress that the Reagan Administration had made insufficient effort to persuade other countries to adopt sanctions. That reluctance had not been in evidence in other cases—for example, against Cuba, Vietnam, or the Soviet Union—and so the Administration, still opposed to sanctions, was, by inaction, making its prediction of ineffectiveness self-fulfilling.

Other frequent arguments against sanctions are patronizing or short-sighted. An expanding economy has brought some improvement to South African blacks, but it has made no dent on the item of dispute: political power. Sanctions alone did not lead the Rhodesian government to the negotiating table. But sanctions weakened Rhodesia, causing it to open inefficient industries; to pay middle men exorbitant costs for imports while receiving low payments for exports; and to risk serious shortages of spare parts. It was said that one could buy almost any consumer good off the shelf in Rhodesia. What was not said was at what price. Most important, a sanctions-weakened Rhodesia was eventually in no position to resist the increasing toll of war.

Sanctions, then, must be evaluated in both the short term and long term. On both scores, there is some evidence of effect. In the short term, sanctions played a part in shaking confidence in the South African economy, in reducing new investment, and in pushing South Africa's rate of economic growth (less than 3 percent in 1987) below the level needed (4-5 percent) to provide new jobs for a growing population.[1] In a development not seen since the days of the "poor white" Afrikaners in the 1930s, whites have joined the unemployment lines.

Some of the impact of sanctions has been masked by developments that have nothing to do with the South African economy, such as the higher price of gold and the ability of

South Africans to purchase the business of departing Americans at fire sale prices. However, South Africa is still faced with the fact that it needs foreign investment and is heavily dependent on the export of raw materials and the import of technology. As Dr. Gerhard de Kock, Governor of the South African Reserve Bank, put it in September 1987 statement:

> The basic underlying problems that threaten to isolate us from the rest of the world have not yet been solved. The outflow of capital, the emigration of skilled people, the large discount on the financial rand, and the decline in fixed and inventory investment, are all sending us messages that we should heed.

Perhaps the most difficult anti-sanctions arguments to refute is their harm, at least in the short term, to the black population, raising the prospect of an economically crippled South Africa, an inauspicious start for a new government. This argument is eloquently expressed by, among others, Helen Suzman, a courageous and outspoken opponent of apartheid. In Europe, Prime Minister Thatcher has cited the Suzman argument on occasion. The argument is true, but it ignores the sentiment among Africans in support of sanctions. More importantly, it ignores the root argument for sanctions: that they are a way to avoid escalating violence, with its devastating effect on the economy and the lives of blacks and whites alike. To join this argument it would have to be shown that there is another alternative to violence that shows reasonable promise of bring-ing real change to South Africa.

The sanctions debate would be clearer if three facts were acknowledged:

- We know how to apply sanctions reasonably effectively against South Africa. We have not chosen to do so.
- Sanctions are not always applied for economic effect. Sometimes they are a measure of additional pressure or a demonstration of political support when we are as yet unable or unwilling to take more severe measures to affect the situation. The irony, proven in the case of Rhodesia, is that failure to apply sanctions effectively in situations that

politically or morally demand that we "do something" can
result in ever-escalating sanctions accompanied by violence.
In other words, a tentative approach may have little effect
on the object of sanctions but instead encourage the object
to believe it can act with impunity, eventually making it
necessary to resort to the sweeping measures the original
approach sought to avoid.
- Even the strongest opponents of sanctions tend to support
  them under extreme provocation. Thus the British supported sanctions against Rhodesia and eventually against Libya
  and Iran.

Is the Sanctions Debate Irrelevant?

The sanctions debate is not just simplistic; it is increasingly
irrelevant. For years the international business community
resisted demands for sanctions on the grounds that they were
political and so beyond the competence of business. However,
the actions that business so steadfastly resisted on political
grounds have been increasingly taken on economic grounds. In
1985, 1986 and 1987, the number of American firms withdrawing from South Africa was 40, 50, and 55, respectively. Exact
figures for European companies are not available but they were
significantly smaller.

Most companies that withdrew gave economic reasons for
doing so, but in 1985, political and economic factors had become
so interwoven as to be inseparable. Political unrest led to
depressed economic conditions with little prospect that political
conditions would improve markedly soon. Moreover, particularly in the United States, investors found their domestic business
prospects in jeopardy as a result of actions by individuals,
shareholder groups, and local or state governments. Thus, while
the immediate reason for withdrawal might have been economic,
the root cause was political.

These withdrawals of foreign investment from South Africa
will continue if there is no fundamental change in that country.
To be sure, American and European investors have concluded
that they can continue to realize profits from South Africa
without the political and economic risks of direct investment.

They are thus moving toward the long established Japanese formula of licenses, agents, and franchises but no investment. Yet even this approach is not without problems. Political pressure will focus more and more on *any* commercial relationship with South Africa, forcing it to resort to expensive, unscrupulous, and unreliable middle men.

Instead of sanctions, the arguments that usually dominate the debate on South Africa, the real issue facing the United States and the Western alliance in South and southern Africa is the need for unified action. Whether in the United Nations, in the Commonwealth, in other multilateral organizations, or in bilateral relations, South Africa will be more and more on the agenda. South Africa's intransigence reduces the ability of the United States and of its allies to argue that the passage of time is hopeful for a favorable resolution without a further deterioration of the situation. The Commonwealth is sharply divided with Britain apparently in a minority of one and, frustratingly, the other members unable to budge the current British government. In the European Community, the situation is somewhat different: Britain finds some support from West Germany, and perhaps, tacitly, France, but the Netherlands, Denmark, and others prefer stronger measures. And within NATO there is a similar fissure that would loom larger if the Reagan Administration or its successor decided to press the intent of Congress to persuade other countries to take action similar to those already taken by the United States.

As is the case with the Commonwealth, there is no sign that the failure of Western countries to agree on policies toward South Africa will lead to a split in NATO. The importance of other issues on which the NATO members are united all but eliminates that possibility. That is true despite past policy differences—on the pipeline from the Soviet Union, or on sales of sensitive products to Eastern bloc countries, to cite recent examples in East-West relations. Similarly, in the late 1960s, American relations with some of its European allies chafed under the refusal of the United States to allow the sale to South Africa of light aircraft containing American parts.

However, the failure of the Western countries to present a united front is of far greater importance to what happens in South Africa and the southern Africa region. Just as Rhodesia was able to survive in part because of the assistance of South Africa and Portugal, so South Africa is assisted by the disarray in the West. That failure is supplemented by South Africa's ability to turn to Taiwan and Israel. It is significant that the most encouraging progress on the Namibia issue was made when the then five Western members of the United Nations Security Council, acting together in the Contact Group, negotiated Security Council Resolution 435. Even suspicious African countries tempered their rhetoric and cooperated with the undertaking. Similarly, the Namibia effort broke down when it became clear that the Contact Group would not be united in the face of a flat South African refusal to continue to cooperate. Subsequently, the division grew wider when the United States unilaterally linked a Cuban withdrawal from Angola to the Namibia settlement. Thus ended a unique, highly successful experiment in Western cooperation and began, once again, an unrestrained pursuit of selfish objectives in Namibia by the South African government.

The significance of united action cannot be overemphasized. South Africa enjoys decided advantages over those who oppose its policy. However misguided, South African objectives are clear; its strategy enjoys support within its government; and there is continuity in the implementation of its policy. On the other hand, there is no united policy among the allies other than the rhetoric of abhorrence to apartheid, and even that was in dispute in the early Reagan years. Execution of policy swings wildly when parties exchange power in Britain, France, and the United States. Each new administration must learn the intricate maneuvers of delay and obfuscation that South African officials have perfected over many years. All too frequently, there is at least one government of the alliance that takes office under the illusion that South Africa will change by gentle persuasion, and only later comes to face harsh reality.

Clearly, what is needed is a realistic appraisal of the situation in South Africa and a coordinated strategy to deal with it. It is not in the interest of the West to see young South Africans become increasingly anti-Western, anti-American, and anti-capitalist. Nor is it in the interest of the West to see the situation in South Africa or the region deteriorate to the point that it faces the turmoil of previous instance—Iran, the Philippines, Nicaragua, Cuba, Angola, or Haiti—when change, long-delayed, finally took place. The lesson of those cases is that the value that a failure to act purports to save will eventually suffer a more jolting and probably longer-lasting blow; the human cost of inaction, in social and political turmoil, can be incalculable.

United action would put the West tactically on the same playing field as South Africa. It would introduce a sense of direction, making any measures, small or large, more effective. Potential strain in U.S.-European relations would be removed. South Africans would be less likely to count on Western divisions in calculating the consequences of their own failure to act. While none of these steps would in themselves decisively alter the situation in South Africa, they could make a positive contribution toward change.

Note

1. *Economist*, August 22, 1987.

Glossary

In writing about South Africa, language itself poses a problem. In this book we, for convenience, use the South African government's racial categories, and in general omit quotation marks around them as unnecessary clutter, but that usage implies no recognition of those categories.

African
Under South African law, the word is a racial classification that encompasses the majority of the population of South Africa. It refers to any person "who is, or is generally accepted as, a member of any aboriginal race or tribe of Africa."

Afrikaner
A South African white descended from the early Dutch, German or Huguenot settlers who immigrated to South Africa in the seventeenth century.

ANC
The African National Congress is the continent's oldest liberation movement. Organized in 1912, the ANC has led the fight of black South Africans for equality and political rights. Outlawed in 1960 after the Sharpeville uprising, its leaders were imprisoned or forced into exile.

BLS states
Botswana, Lesotho, and Swaziland.

Banning
An action taken by the minister of justice under the authority of the Internal Security Act to restrict an individual's freedom of movement, association, and expression. Organizations and publications can also be banned.

Blacks
As used in this book, a collective noun including Africans, Coloureds, Indians, and other Asians.

Boer	A white South African of Dutch, German or Huguenot descent. Sometimes a synonym for Afrikaner.
Broederbond	An exclusive, male-only secret organization established in 1918 to promote the interests of Afrikaners. This group was instrumental in the creation of the National Party in 1934.
Coloured	A racial classification denoting South Africans of mixed race, mainly African-European descent. A coloured person is sometimes defined as one who is not a white or an African; a definition that can include Indians and Asians.
Commonwealth	A voluntary association of 49 sovereign states linking former members of the British Empire.
Community Councils	Local government bodies of elected black officials with limited powers over black urban areas.
COSATU	The Congress of South African Trade Unions emerged in 1983 as the largest union federation with some 500,000, predominately African, members.
EPG	The Eminent Persons Group established at the Commonwealth Heads of Government meeting in 1985 sought to encourage a process of political dialogue in South Africa. Co-chaired by Malcolm Fraser and General Olusegun Obasanjo, the findings of the group were published under the title, *Mission to South Africa: The Commonwealth Report*.
European Communities	The EC is the collective designation of the twelve-state European Steel and Coal Community, European Economic Community, and the European Atomic Energy Community.

Front Line States	Angola, Botswana, Mozambique, Tanzania, Zambia, and Zimbabwe constitute a loose political grouping formed in the 1970's to deal with regional security issues.
Group Areas Act	Law that governs ownership and occupation in specific geographic areas according to race.
Homelands	Areas designated by the South African government as homes for the various African ethnic groups. The ten homelands are: Bophuthatswana, the Ciskei, Gazankulu, KaNgwane, KwaZulu, Lebowa, Ndebele, Qwaqwa, the Transkei and Venda.
Inkatha	Founded in 1928 as a Zulu cultural organization, Inkatha was revived in 1974 by Chief Mangosuthu Buthelezi as a *"national* cultural organization," that "desires to abolish all forms of discrimination and separation." The organization claims a membership of one million, predominately Zulus. Inkatha has strained relations with the ANC and the UDF. This internecine struggle among anti-apartheid groups has led to violent clashes between supporters of Inkatha and the UDF.
National Party	The dominant political party in South Africa. The National Party adopted the policy of apartheid in 1945 and came to power in 1948. It has won every national election since then by large margins.
SADCC	The Southern African Development Coordination Council, consisting of the Front Line States, Lesotho, Malawi, and Swaziland was organized to promote closer regional cooperation and to lessen its member's economic dependence on South Africa.

UDF   The United Democratic Front formed in 1983 is a coalition of 600 community, labor and religious organizations working for the peaceful abolition of apartheid. The political activities of the UDF were banned in February 1988.